Pieces

Lessons from the Story of
THE PRODIGAL SON

Printed in the United States of America

ISBN: 978-0-9834584-0-1 PBK.

ISBN: 978-0-9834584-1-8 HBK.

CONTENTS

FOREWORD

When I was a religious newspaper editor in Maryland, I was privileged to have **Lewis McDonald** as my pastor and preacher. I heard him preach ten consecutive sermons on Jesus' parable, *"The Prodigal Son."* What amazed me was he did not repeat himself. A few years after I moved to Tennessee to become the editor of another newspaper, I learned Lewis had preached at least ten more sermons on this parable and still did not repeat himself. I am one of many who pleaded with him to publish some of these sermons. I often prayed that he would. **Pieces** is the answer to my prayer. These sermons touched my life, because they revealed some of the depths of my heavenly Father's love I had not grasped.

William Fletcher Allen

Pieces is not just about Jesus' great story, "The Prodigal Son." It is about you and me, too, because there is a prodigal in all of us. My own life was one so scattered in pieces that I could not begin to find them. But Someone found them. A Carpenter.

CHAPTER ONE
The Loving Father
Luke 15:11-32

Jesus' story of "The Prodigal Son" is by far the greatest story I have ever heard. I know of no other story that speaks so deeply to my heart. I am not thinking only of biblical stories, but all stories. It is a universal story in that people of many languages and cultures have read it or heard it. It is a living story because it has done more than survive. It still lives, and it has the ring of eternity in it. I look for it to be told in heaven. I mean that!

But in the truest sense it should not have been called "The Story of the Prodigal Son." Whoever gave it this label was in error. I have read that the early Church titled Jesus' parables by their first lines, so this story was named "A Certain Man Had Two Sons."

That is closer to the truth, for this parable is "The Parable of the Loving Father." It does not begin, "A certain youth had a father and an older brother." It is really a story about a father who loved his two sons and wanted them to love each other.

Both sons break his heart. Both. The younger son breaks his heart by asking for his share of the inheritance early so he can go live in a far country. By "live" I really mean live it up. Though we do not know of all his sins in the far country, we do know he put no restraints on himself. And no one was there to put restraints on him. So no doubt he satisfied all his desires. More than that, he probably satisfied all his lusts. He wallowed in selfishness. He might have called some of his actions freedom. He might even have called some of it love, even though in the depth of his heart – with which he seldom, if ever, communicated-- he knew his father would call it sin. But to him sin was an irrelevant word.

That is, until he ran out of money and luck and had to take a job feeding swine. A Jewish kid feeding swine! They might as well have branded his forehead, "A Number-One Loser!"

He was at the bottom, rock bottom. Or should I say "slop bottom"!

There at the bottom, the story says, "He came to himself." Why does it take that for a man to come to himself? Sin can be such a mystery.

Grace, however, is a greater mystery: the father running to forgive his boy. If you are aware of the prayer book used by the Episcopal Church for the service of the reconciliation of the penitent, you know the service ends with a quotation from the parable of the prodigal son. After the repentant one has confessed his sins and promised to return to the Lord, the priest lays a hand on the repentant's head to absolve him in the name of God saying, "Now there is rejoicing in heaven, for you were lost and are found; you were dead and now you are alive…" They are wonderful words, and it is a magnificent sacrament, but it is out of context. Before the son in this story can say a single word of confession, the father sees the son on the road and runs to forgive him.

Remember, this is God running. This is grace on its feet. Since this father wears a long robe – more like a modern woman's long dress than a modern man's trousers – he has to pull up his robe to run. In the Middle East this means the loss of all dignity. This is God running without dignity to reach his sinful son as quickly as he can.

Some years ago a Chinese artist who was a new Christian painted this father running, and in the painting the father's two shoes don't match. They are not even the same color. When a friend asked the artist about the shoes which did not match, the artist gave this explanation:

> Because the father is so overjoyed to see his son coming home that he grabs the two nearest shoes and puts them on and runs to meet him. He doesn't care that the shoes don't match. [1]

A father running with mismatched shoes and not even the same color. And it is not the run of a young sprinter but of an old man with his robe pulled up. There is no dignity in his running, and his running almost looks clumsy. But outside the stable in Bethlehem where Jesus was born and the cross in Jerusalem where he died, we probably will not find anywhere else a greater word picture of the love of God than this old man running. That is why this great parable is really the story of the loving God rather than the story of the prodigal son.

The Scripture, however, reminds us that this father had two sons, and so the story is not complete until we give our attention to the older son. When the younger son came home, the older son didn't know it, for he was in the fields working. After all, he was the dependable son.

At the end of the work day as he started home, he learned from a servant that his brother had come home and his father was giving a party in his brother's honor. When he learned this, he refused to go in. He just stood there in the field near the house. To say he was disgusted would be a great understatement. He was livid! He was a thousand times more angry than he had ever been in all his life.

I suppose it is not easy to be the oldest child in a family, because it is the oldest child who has to break in parents. We don't know how to be parents until the first child breaks us in. I spanked my older son more than I spanked my second son. This did not mean my second son did not deserve as many spankings. I remember a day when I came home from the office and my wife met me at the door with our second son. She pointed a finger at him and said two words: "Kill him!" I said to her, "Dear, could you give me three minutes to develop a real hatred for him first?"

I had mellowed in the passing of time. I spanked my third son even fewer times than I spanked his older brothers. This did not mean the youngest son was an angel. It only meant I had mellowed more.

Surely Steven, our oldest son, was aware of this because he was always trying to get David, the second son, in trouble. When I punished David, his punishment was merely words: "David, I am disappointed in you!" If those words hurt at all, they only hurt David's heart; whereas, I had hurt Steven's bottom.

Of course there were moments I spent with Steven that were full of love. Some of them Steven was too young to remember. For instance, one evening I saved him from drowning. This is the son I spanked the most. And there was the day when at the risk of my own life, I pushed him out of the way of a speeding car. This is the son I spanked the most. And I am quite sure I cared more about his well-being when he was an infant and a toddler than I cared about the two younger sons. I feel parents probably panic more with their first child when the child's well-being is threatened. I recall preparing a sermon one day in my study when Steven was an infant. Suddenly I heard my wife scream, "Steven just fell out of his bed!" Tossing papers, books and pen to the desk and floor, I rushed to Steven's room. By the time a third child comes along, such a fall doesn't even faze you. When you hear him fall out of bed, you simply look up for a moment and say to yourself, "That's too bad."

I also spent more time with my oldest son in his early years than I did with the other two sons when they were young. After all, he was my only child then. I didn't have to divide my time with the other two. Steven and I spent quality time with each other. We did so many things together. Precious memories. I will not forget them. They will live in my heart forever. Still, I don't think it is easy to be the oldest son. There probably are responsibilities, sensitivities, and demands the other sons will never know and understand. There are also self-imposed pressures that only the oldest son can feel.

Learning that his older son is standing out in the field refusing to come to the party, the father in Jesus' parable leaves the house and goes out to his son. This means the father took the initiative with both sons. He ran down the road to one and walked through the fields to the other. Finding his son in the field, the father asks him, "Is there a problem? Why are you missing the party?"

"Oh, yes! There is a big problem," his son responds. "All these years I have served you, never throwing away your money in sinful living, yet not even once have you given a party in my honor."

His father says, "Son, what is the matter with you? You need to get your head on straight. How can you say I've never given you anything when all that I have is yours?" Let us remember, this is God talking. The same God who ran to greet and forgive the younger son tells his older son, "Son, all that I have is yours!"

Isn't that enough? All the resources of God. What do we require? How much do we think we deserve?

"Son, all that I have is yours. I have made that clear in so many, many ways. How have you missed it?"

The contrast in the lives of the two sons is stated eloquently by H. Stephen Shoemaker.

> There are many sad things in this world: to live your lives in repetitive, self-defeating behaviors, running from God and from self and from anybody who might know you, living in hiding, never coming home. But perhaps this is the saddest: to try to buy what can only be given, to try to earn what is yours already, to search the world over for a treasure buried in your own backyard, to live forever trying to earn God's love and never discover that it is a gift as free as the sun that shines and the rain that falls from the skies. [2]

The older son's sin lies in what he thought he deserved. Whereas his younger brother's sin was recklessness, his sin was righteousness. Self-righteousness. Jesus taught us that no one is so far from God as the self-righteous. The older son thought what he deserved gave him the right to be judgmental and critical, especially toward his brother.

The older son grieved his father because he couldn't and wouldn't forgive his younger brother. If we think this parable was about only one son, the younger, who hurt his father, we have missed the whole truth. It is really a story about two sons who hurt their father. Our unwillingness to forgive brings its own pain to the great heart of God.

Maybe there is someone you can't forgive. A bitterness you cannot let go. Is there someone you don't think deserves your forgiveness? Do you realize you cannot forgive anyone more than your heavenly Father has forgiven you? That is why Jesus taught us to pray, *"Forgive us our trespasses as we forgive…"*

When Sybil Canon was a teenager, she lived in a small town in Mississippi. She was recognized as the outstanding youth in her church. She was a featured soloist at a revival and president of the youth group.

Her Uncle Chester and Aunt Mattie lived with Sybil and her family. Chester was not a Christian. He was known as "the town drunk." One morning when Uncle Chester was in the kitchen frying bacon, Sybil, having had all the embarrassment she could take from him, screamed at him: "Your wife has to support you, and everybody in Iuka laughs at you. You can't walk straight! You can't talk without slurring and slobbering, and you smell like a gutter. I can't stand having you in my mother's house. I can't stand seeing Aunt Mattie put up with you. The truth is, I can't stand you! Do you know what you are, Uncle Chester? You're a drunk, a worthless drunk!"

Uncle Chester, never looking up from his frying pan, said softly, "Sybil, I know what I am, but do you know what you are?" Sybil Canon will tell you today that this question changed her life. For the first time since becoming a Christian, she looked honestly at her own Christianity, and she decided it was too full of pride, with little compassion.

She changed. She gave up her own righteousness and replaced it with love and forgiveness.[3]

I must confess something here. It is fun to hate Pharisees. I believe the elder son in the story was a Pharisee. Jesus even aimed the story of the elder brother at Pharisees. They heard and knew it, but nothing in their thought or acts changed. They remained self-righteous. Oh, it is so much fun to hate them.

In all previous sermons I have preached on the elder brother, I have been very hard on him. I know of no other preacher who has been so critical of him. I cannot stand self-righteousness.

I must confess, however, that in all those other sermons about him I never saw him through his father's eyes or his father's heart. The eyes of grace and the heart of love. I was ashamed of myself, and I asked God to forgive me.

There is no easy way to lose a son you love. I don't know how I would cope if I lost one of my three sons. The father in the story did not want to lose a son either to his own recklessness or his own righteousness. So the father hoped his older son would accept the invitation to come on in from the fields to the homecoming party. Wouldn't it be a great sadness if one son made it home from the far country, but the other did not make it home from the nearby fields?

Jesus did not tell us at the end of the story whether the older son accepted his father's invitation. Perhaps this omission is Jesus' way of saying that the choice to love is a choice each of us must make. But make no mistake! The Father wants us home, and the Father has gone as far as love can go to get us home.

You see, this is the story of the loving father.

CHAPTER TWO
You Can Go Home Again
Luke 15:15-17

Long ago Thomas Wolfe, North Carolina's proud son, penned a novel with the now famous title, *You Can't Go Home Again.* That, of course, is quite true. In the world in which we live it is more true than ever in human history because of the radical changes taking place in our generation. The space age has changed more than space. It has changed home.

The road in front of our church is an excellent example of such change. If you lived on this road when the church was founded in 1932, you probably lived on a farm. If you still own this land, it is likely no longer a farm. It's a service station or a doctor's office or a fast food restaurant or a shopping center or an enormous apartment complex or a bank or a college. A farm it is not. You can't go home again.

Not only is it true that you cannot go home again because of environmental changes, but you can't go home again once you leave home for a considerable period of time because of changes in one's lifetime goals. If a child leaves home to attend college and only comes home for holidays and for the summer, it is not quite the same home. As someone said, what once was the place where the heart turned at the end of each day has become a stop-off place on the road to somewhere else. You can't go home again.

So Thomas Wolfe was right. He was also wrong. The truth is, by the grace of God, you can go home again. You can go back to the Father in this parable. Not only can we, but for our sake we must. We must all go back to this One who gave us life.

He is the Source – the source of every good thing that has happened to us. He is more than that. He is the source of life itself, for we came into being by Him and through Him. We would never have lived at all had He not willed it. We are His children – His sons and His daughters – and no matter how far the country to which we flee, and no matter how deep the sin in which we wallow, we cannot get away from the source of our lives. He is the vine from which we branches grow. He is the sea toward which we rivers flow. He is both the Past and the Future. He is Yesterday, Today, and Tomorrow. He is both Creator and Redeemer. In creation He showed His hand; in redemption He showed His heart. He is the Lover of our spirits. He is Sunrise and Sunset. He is Fall, Winter, Spring, and Summer. He is the Seasons of our years. In regard to His identity, He said it best Himself through the prophet Isaiah, *Turn to me and be saved, all you ends of the earth; for I am God, and there is no other* (Isaiah 45:22).

C. S. Lewis in his book, *Mere Christianity*, provided a profound insight as to life with the Source:

> A car is made to run on gasoline, and it would not run properly on anything else. Now God designed the human machine to run on Himself. He Himself is the fuel our spirits were designed to burn, or the food our spirits were designed to feed on. There is no other. [4]

Because there is no other, the father in our parable could give his son the youth's inheritance to take to the far country, but he could not give him joy in the far country apart from Himself. It is not there. You must go home again!

I wish I could convince every prodigal – whether young or old – that no matter how much money and other resources you take with you to the far country, you will go bankrupt there in regard to life's meaning and purpose.

No matter how many hopes and dreams you take with you to the far country, sooner or later you will find yourself in a pig's pen called hopelessness. In the distant land you will come to a dead end.

And the word *dead* in *dead end* is almost the perfect word to explain the youth's fate in the far country, because dead is one of the words Jesus used to describe what happened to the boy in the far country. At the boy's home-coming the father says to some of his servants, *"For this son of mine was dead and is alive again...."* He wasn't really dead was he? Had his heart stopped beating at some moment in the far country? No, but he was dead because the real life was at home.

We must go back to the Source of our lives. We must also go back to the One who is the Blesser of our lives. The Father's blessing is a necessity to experience real living. In sin's far country, for our lives to have ultimate meaning and true joy, we must have His blessing. His stamp of approval. His best wishes. His Godspeed.

Years ago there was a show on television entitled *Father Knows Best*. I liked it because I thought it was a great mix of family values with some comedy. The show was fictitious, of course, but there is a Father who knows best. Always. In every situation. Every step of the way. Not only does He know what is best for all of us, He wants what is best. I think we all at times have difficulty believing that.

We live in a day of broken relationships, and we tend to think we can get along in our lives not dealing with these broken relationships. The truth, however, is that there will always be something missing in our lives until these shattered separations are restored and redeemed to the best of our abilities.

Laurens Van der Post told a story about two brothers who lived in South Africa. The elder was tall, strong, good looking, highly intelligent and an incredible athlete. When he was old enough, he was sent away from home to a prestigious private school in the homeland where he became the popular and admired leader of the entire student body.

His younger brother was neither good looking nor athletic. He was a hunchback. He was by no means skilled in most things, but he did have one great gift. He had a magnificent singing voice.

Eventually, this younger brother became a student at the same school where his brother was a student. But the elder brother did not let anyone at the school know that he was the hunchback's brother. One day in a cruel outbreak of mob violence, a group of students ganged up on the younger brother, jeering at him and tearing off his shirt to reveal his deformed back.

The elder brother was aware of what was going on because he saw the scene from the chemistry lab where he was working on an assignment. He could have gone out and faced these sadistic students and told the mob that this hunchback was his brother. Had he done that, he probably could have stopped the harassment because of his athleticism and popularity, but he chose to remain in the chemistry lab.

The younger brother was never the same after that. He left the school and returned home to work on his parents' farm. He kept to himself and spent much time alone, and he stopped singing. Completely stopped. Meanwhile his brother had become a soldier in World War II and was stationed in Palestine. One night, as he lay outdoors gazing into a starlit sky, he remembered what he had done – or not done – for his brother at the private school. He was ashamed of himself, and he realized he would never have peace of mind and heart until he went home and asked his brother for forgiveness. So he made the difficult and risky wartime journey from Palestine to South Africa and confronted his brother. The brothers talked long into the night as the elder brother confessed his great guilt and remorse. They cried together and embraced, and the breach between them was healed.

Something else happened that night. The older brother had fallen asleep when he was startled awake by the sound of a full, rich and magnificent voice that sang out into the night. [5]

You can go home again, and when you reach home, you must confess the unlove in your past and repent. If we don't go home and confess our unlove and repent, we will miss some of the most wonderful experiences that could be ours. Like the beauty of joy. The elder brother stayed in the chemistry lab while his brother was treated so cruelly. We have all done worse. We remained hidden in a lab or somewhere else the day a good man was killed on a cruel cross on a rugged hill. There can be no deep blessing in our lives until we deal with this.

The young man in the parable had missed the blessing, and I think this is the greatest reason why his father hurt when his son left home. It is one thing to hurt when a son you love so much is far from home, when you know that in the far away land your son is truly happy, filled with true joy and truly blessed. You can cope with that. You may cry a lot, but you can cope.

But it is quite another thing when you know your son in the distant land has never known life's greatest blessing and the great deep of love. That is the unbearable hurt – when a son in the far country has rejected both the Source and the Blesser. To phrase it another way, to know your son has rejected not only his God, but his Father. It is a terrible hurt to know the journey of your son will end in emptiness.

But if you are in that emptiness now, that lonely emptiness, like a prodigal son down to being less than a slave-laborer and craving food for swine, I have some very good news for you. Thomas Wolfe was wrong. You can go home again.

CHAPTER THREE
You Don't Have to Make It Home
Luke 15:18a

"**If** I can just make it home…" How ironic that this had become this young man's obsession. "If I can just make it home…" How strange that this now was the greatest longing of his life. "If I can just make it home…" It is almost impossible to believe that the greatest desire of his heart is to make it home.

If there were ever a boy who wanted to get away from home, this was the boy. That had been his daily obsession and his never-ending dream. "If I can just get away from home." Day and night that wish had absorbed both his mind and his heart. "If I can just get away from home…" It was all he had wanted. It was all he had needed. It was the fulfillment of all his dreams.

Why did he want to get away from home? Perhaps it was because there was so much hard work to do in the fields and barns. And surely he wanted to get away from his very religious and legalistic older brother. He was a jerk. He was even more of a jerk than the local pastor. It makes sense to me that he wanted to get away from the demanding work at home and from his self-righteous brother.

But I don't understand why he wanted to get away from his father. There is nothing in the story to tell us why, except that he wanted to sin. (Isn't that why we want to get away from his Father?)

23

It must have hurt his father deeply. Hurt like hell. For the boy's wish and attitude and mind-set were heartless rejection of the home in which he had been born and nurtured. He turns his back on tradition. But more than that, he turns his back on his father.

The boy didn't just want to leave home temporarily in order to see more of the world. He wanted to leave home for the rest of his life.

This doesn't even begin to tell how much his leaving crushed his dad. Luke jumps into the story so quickly and with such swift sentences that we almost overlook the greatest hurt to his father when taken in the setting of that day and that tradition. He asks his father, actually he demands, for his share of his father's estate immediately. In that culture a son only received his part of the father's wealth upon the death of the father. In rare exceptions when a father shared his wealth prior to his own death, the father was allowed to live off the proceeds of the estate until his death. I mean, the old man can't live on nothing. This was before Social Security with its wonderful retirement plan!

This boy wants all he has coming now. Before sunset. So he takes his share of the inheritance and he leaves home. Forever. He might as well have looked his father in the face and said, "Old Man, I really wish you were dead!"

It was an unbelievable request in his day, and even today, almost 2000 years later, it would still be an unbelievable request in Israel. Kenneth Bailey has researched this matter of tradition in today's world extensively, and he wrote this:

> For over fifteen years I have been asking people of all walks of life from Morocco to India and from Turkey to the Sudan about the implications of a son's request for his inheritance while the father is still living. The answer has always been emphatically the same…the conversation runs as follows:
>
> "Has anyone ever made such a request in your village?"
> "Never!"

"Could anyone ever make such a request?"

"Impossible!"

"If anyone ever did, what would happen?"

"His father would beat him, of course!"

"Why?"

"The request means he wants his father to die." [6]

If his father's dying was what was necessary to get away from home, then so be it. "If I can just get away from home…" This was his goal. His dream. His want. His everything.

So, how ironic it is that making it home had become this young man's obsession. He ached for home. This was what he wanted more than anything else in his world.

Because in the far country he at last learned the real truth about the far country, which is to say he learned the real truth about sin. Philip Bailey was a nineteenth-century poet. At some time during my educational process I was required to study his poetry. Unfortunately his poetry never moved me, so I chose to forget it. But I do remember two sentences of his prose. I cannot forget them even if I try. They ring with too much truth about sin: "The first and worst of all frauds is to cheat one's self. All sin is easy after that."

I also remember the old English couplet which I believe to be true: "Still as of old, man by himself is priced; for thirty pieces [Judas] sold himself, not Christ."

The prodigal son sold himself. That is what really hurt the father when his son left home.

It wasn't so much that his son wanted him dead, although that must have hurt. The greater hurt was that his father knew in the far country that his son would sell himself.

And so he did. He lost everything he took with him. His money was his least valuable asset. But since money is such a tangible, surface reality, it is the easiest and most simple way to measure what he lost. He lost all his money.

His appearance was the first sign of the loss. His tattered rags and his frail body. This boy who once had resembled his father in his looks and his dress now looks worse than his father's hired servants. The hired servant in those days was just a notch above being a slave. The boy who had been a son is now a slave!

One of the signs of his slavery was that he was barefooted. In the South before the Civil War, most slaves were barefooted. It was a sign of their poverty and their position. Shoes were for masters and white folks. They longed for shoes. An old spiritual says it all: "All of God's chillun got shoes. When I get to hebben I'm gonna put on my shoes; I'm gonna walk all ovah God's hebben." The boy, once a son, is now a slave.

But his condition is worse than that. He is an animal. The only job he can find during the depression that swept the far country is feeding pigs! And he is so very hungry that he craves pig's food! He is like an animal. This young man who was made in the image of God is like an animal.

But there is an even greater tragedy than being like a slave and an animal. He has become a lost person. Verse 24 almost implies it is better to be dead than to be lost. After embracing his son on the road upon his son's return from the far country, the father says to his servants, "This my son was dead, and is alive again." One would think the father would stop there with no additional word. I mean, what can you add after you say someone is dead? Yet, the father adds this word: "He was lost, and is found."

Is it worse to be lost than to be dead? You might ask O. J. Simpson. In a line many believed to be a suicide note he wrote, "Please think of the real O. J. and not this lost person." [7]

It is all strange to me. The boy who wanted his father dead is dead himself. The boy who left home for the far country to find his life there lost his life there. Paul Scherer defines the point of death as "the point where life ceases to have any meaning for you." (On those terms I wonder how many reading this book are at the point of death?)

G. K. Chesterton once said, "The fall of Man means…whatever I am, I am not myself." The boy in Luke was no longer himself. He was more than dead. He was lost.

But the story says the boy "came to himself." This is grace at the depths! He was about as deep in emptiness as one can go when he came to himself. At such depths in one's life only grace can bring one to himself. It was his father's grace that brought him to himself, for there is no grace except the grace of his Father. We can love someone, even many, but we can never have grace toward anyone. This means his father was with him in the far country. I am not suggesting the boy knew his father was with him, for he didn't even know if his father was still alive. (Just as sometimes we don't know his Father is with us and that his Father will never die.)

The boy came to himself and said to himself, "If I can just make it home…" Home. Woven deeply in our lives is the longing for home. In "Little Gidding" T. S. Eliot in these incredible words wrote:

We shall not cease from exploration

And the end of all our exploring

Will be to arrive where we started

And know the place for the first time.

Those who have experiences working with the homeless will be quick to tell you that homelessness is much more than homelessness. It is home-sickness. Lance Morrow in an essay in TIME wrote about the "mystery of home." He tells about a man named Ernest who lived in a park outside Phoenix. In the park he had built a home out of cardboard boxes. He had interlocked the boxes in a creative way so that they kept out the cold Arizona nights. Morrow, whom Ernest permitted to enter the boxes, found them warm, safe, and in their own way, cozy. They also provided some privacy. What most people did not know about Ernest is that he had been a highly salaried and highly trusted engineer for Boeing, Inc. So we have to call Ernest's situation more than homelessness.

I think Ernest was trying to make it home. The longing for home is rooted deeply in our lives. More deeply than we know.

"I'll be home for Christmas" are words in a familiar Christmas song, as though Christmas will not be Christmas if we don't make it home. The song closes with the words, "I'll be home for Christmas if only in my dreams," as if to say we will make it home, if in no other way, in our dreams. Our dreams are never far from home.

This yearning for home even shows up in our national pastime – baseball. Why don't they call it fourth base instead of home? They call the others first base, second base, and third base. So why don't they call the final destination fourth base? Because even in play we call it home, or maybe, it is home that calls us. Sam Keen, psychologist and author, in his book, *The Passionate Life*, writes, "To love is to return to a home we never left, to remember who we are."[8]

"If I can just make it home…" the prodigal son kept saying to himself. But to his overwhelming surprise, he didn't have to make it home. He just had to make it to the place where his father ran to meet him.

The fact is the boy didn't make it home. At least, not all the way. When he was still a long way off, his father saw him and ran to meet him and embrace him with grace. Keep in mind this was the father he had wanted dead!

None of us have to make it home. We only have to get to the place where the Father runs to meet us. That place has a name. It is called Calvary.

The Father God was not really absent from Calvary as some teach. He knew when it happened. He wasn't preoccupied with something else. He didn't sleep through it. In 2 Corinthians 5:19 Paul reminds us that *God was in Christ* on the Cross.

The Father God – running father in the parable – at Calvary was naked so that we prodigals might have his robe, the robe of grace. He wore no family ring at Calvary so that we might wear his ring and be his sons and daughters forever. And at Calvary he is barefooted so that we can wear his shoes and be free. Free to be ourselves. Our real selves.

You don't have to make it home. You just have to make it to Calvary, the place where the father runs to meet you. Can you make it to Calvary? I don't mean in geographical distance. I mean in faith. In repentance, and more than anything else, in love.

An old hymn written back in 1906 by Jessie B. Pounds is entitled *"The Way of the Cross Leads Home."* Yes, and it is the only way that does, so you don't have to make it home. You just have to make it to the cross of Jesus.

CHAPTER FOUR
No Longer Worthy
Luke 15:19a

This is an ancient story, but it is also a modern story. It is a story of grandeur, but it is also a story of the gutter. It is a story about wishes, longings and dreams, but it is also a story about reality. It is a story about great unlove, but it is also a story about the greatest love ever known. And why should we give it a hearing? Because we are in it.

The first characteristic I notice about the young man in the story is his arrogance. In arrogance he tells his father that he wants to give up all his responsibilities and relationships at home and go live in a distant land. This might not be as arrogant today, but in that long-ago world it was rude. Almost everyone lived all their lives in the same place where they were born. Grandparents, parents, children and grandchildren shared the same land all their lives. Not much more than a century ago that was even the pattern in our nation. Few people ever moved away from the area where they were born. But the young man in the story tells his father he is going to live, not in the next county, but in another country.

He tells his father. He doesn't ask his father. There is no question mark. He doesn't say, "May I get my inheritance now and go live in a distant land?" Instead he says, "Give me my money right now." His phrasing is more like an order than a request. He is overwhelmingly arrogant!

He cares for no one but himself. He wants to pretend that this is the day after his father's funeral so he can be in charge of his life. His father's dying means nothing to him. He is too consumed by his own living. And he really enjoys his living in the new country until a day comes when his living collides with reality. The late Paul Tillich gave the best definition of "reality" I ever heard. He said, "Reality is what we have to adjust to because we discover it will not adjust to us."

Reality taught him that, in spite of all his arrogance and knowledge and self-sufficiency, he wasn't very smart. Almost every week of my life I pray for a young man I know who is one of the most brilliant young men I have ever known. And if you are among the few unlearned who don't know how brilliant he is, he himself will tell you about his brilliance. But the brilliant young man is not very smart because he is addicted to drugs. Brilliant arrogance eventually leaves all of us addicted to something. The young man in the distant country became addicted to sin, and it ruined him.

Like reality, life doesn't always adjust to our dreams. At the depths of loneliness the prodigal son said, "I have sinned." It was probably the least arrogant thing he had ever admitted about himself. Oh, the loneliness of arrogance. The stupidity of brilliance. The emptiness of sin.

The irony is that the young man had to be ruined by sin before he ever really knew his father. "I am no longer worthy of being called your son," he said to his father when he returned home. I believe those words were sincere. When he voiced those words – to himself and to his father – it was the first time he really knew he no longer deserved to be called this father's son. He was no longer worthy.

Nor are we. Somewhere in our past we have treated this Father like dirt beneath our feet. Like He didn't even matter. As if He had no feelings. As if His words were stupid. In a little verse with an enormous truth, someone said:

> I lived for myself, I thought for myself,
>
> For myself, and none beside-
>
> Just as if Jesus had never lived,

As if he had never died.

We have all done this. Kyle Haseldon spoke of an equality which seems to be common to all races, cultures and citizens: "Our equality does not lie in the fact that we are as good as each other as much as in the fact that we are as bad as each other and in equal need of redemption."

We have all done this. Mother Teresa said something about her own life that absolutely shocked me. She said she engaged in her ministry of love because she knew there was a Hitler inside her. Mother Teresa said this! We are all guilty. We are all to blame for the arrogance. For insensitivity. For Calvary. Calvary where we didn't just wish He were dead. We killed Him.

What we have done we have done. We can't go back and correct it. We can wish we had not done it, but wishing has never taken the place of reality. We cannot turn our backs on our past or bury our heads in the sand. We cannot escape blame or bury guilt. We must confess it. We must, at last, say it. "I am no longer worthy."

One can ignore the truth for years. Decades. Most of one's life. But the truth will come out. "I am no longer worthy." That is the truth and it hurts. Nothing hurts so much as the truth. But there is something more about truth which needs to be shared, much more. Nothing blesses as much as truth. Untruth never leads to ultimate blessing. Untruth is built upon lies, and given enough time, such a foundation of sand will crumble. The only solid foundation is the truth.

The prodigal son never knew the greatest of all truths until he returned home to tell his father, "I am no longer worthy of being called your son." When his father responded with overwhelming love, the prodigal learned he had been wrong about something all his life. He had thought his standing with his father always rested in his own worth. It never did. Not at the moment of his birth. Not in his infancy or the tender days of childhood. Not in the who-knows-what days of adolescence. Certainly not in the days of freedom in the far country. Their continuing relationship always rested in his father's worth. The father he had deserted.

Pieces

The Law speaks to us about what man has done, but the Gospel speaks to us about what God has done. "I am no longer worthy of being called your son," he said to his father, only to discover that what he had no part in creating, he could not destroy! That is why for me there are few scenes in all the Bible that speak as deeply as this scene where the prodigal returns home and says to his father on the road near home, "I am no longer worthy of being called your son."

His father at that moment speaks to his son who by his own admission says he is worth nothing. The father speaks from his own worth saying what he wishes to give his son out of his great worth: The best robe. A treasured family ring. Shoes. A party in his son's honor. And the greatest treasure of all, forgiveness. What we do not have the power to create, we do not have the power to destroy.

"Father, I am no longer worthy of being called your son."

So? What else is new?

CHAPTER FIVE
Responsible Sons
Luke 15:19b RSV

In this story, which is in my opinion the greatest ever told, Jesus builds the story around two people: a father and a son. So this is a story that deals with a relationship. A father and a son.

This is not a story about a man and an acquaintance (an acquaintanceship). It is not a story about a man and a friend (a friendship). It is not even a story about a relationship because of marriage (husband and wife); instead, it tells of a true relationship because of birth, a father and a son.

So this is a story about a relationship. You will need to keep that in mind throughout the story, lest you miss the whole point of the story. The story is about a father and a son.

One day the son came to his father and said, "Father, give me my part of your estate now, for I want to leave home for a far country." There is no evidence that the father tried to restrain the boy and keep him at home against his will. How could He? This father had the wisdom to know that home could never be home to a boy whose heart was in the far country. So the father gave the boy the money he wanted and let his son go.

The father gave his son what he asked. And that is the reason why we can never blame our heavenly Father for our sins. What do you want God to do?

Pieces

Do you want him to deny every desire of our hearts? Do you want him to so manipulate your mind and heart that you can never be tempted to choose anything that does not please him? Is that what you want God to do? Do you realize that if God did that, then you would no longer be you? You would be it. You would be a thing. But this is not a story about a father and a thing; it is a story about a father and a son. Thus the son is allowed to go to the far country where he wastes both his money (actually his father's money) and his life in sinful living.

One day in this far country this boy comes to himself. That is one of the significant lines in the whole story: *"But when he came to himself he said, 'How many of my father's hired servants have bread enough and to spare, but I perish here with hunger! I will arise and go to my father...'"* (Luke 15:17-18 RSV).

An old proverb says, "When a son has to walk barefooted, he remembers how well he had been treated in his father's house." We may never discover how much home means to us until we leave it.

When this boy in Luke 15 came to himself, he remembered home, and when he remembered home, the strange thing is that he did not remember all those restraints "the old man" imposed on him at home; instead, what he remembered was the kind of food they served at home. It was a lot better than pig food and, of course, pig food was all he had left to eat in the far country. And remember, this is not a story about a man and a pig. This is a story about a father and a son.

So when the boy came to himself, he said, *I have sinned.* That was the turning point in his life, and it is the turning point in every life.

Not only does the boy say, I have sinned, but he also says, or at least plans to say, to his father, "Father, I have sinned against heaven and against you...." That is a most profound admission of guilt: against heaven and against you.

All sin is against heaven and against God. When the Bible tells us to forgive each other for our sins, this forgiving only has the potential to restore a broken human relationship. There is absolutely no power in this forgiveness to save sinners. David, the man after God's own heart, drifted from God at one time in his life. He drifted long enough to commit adultery with Bathsheba and to order the killing of her husband, Uriah. Then a day came when Nathan, God's prophet, confronted David about his sin. David's reaction was to say to Nathan, " I have sinned against the Lord." Strange in a way, isn't it? He committed adultery with Bathsheba and murder against Uriah, but David said I have sinned against the Lord. That is great honesty and great theology. All sin is against our heavenly Father. The young man in a pig's pen finally had the courage and honesty to confront the truth: Father, I have sinned against heaven and against you... So the boy who had come to himself and acknowledged his sin turns toward the long road that will lead home. I suppose there is a time to leave home, but there is also a time to come home. I credit the boy for realizing that. I think it is a mark of responsibility, just as I commend him for coming to himself and confessing his sin. These are marks of responsibility.

But, as he journeys home, listen to him as he rehearses the speech he will make to his father upon arriving home, for it is not a mark of responsibility: *"Treat me as one of your hired servants"* (Luke 15:19). He has prepared this beautiful speech, filled with so many sincere and honest words, Father, I have sinned against heaven and against you; I am no longer worthy to be called your son... And that is where he should have ended his speech; but no, he adds this stupid line, Treat me as one of your hired servants.

Of course, that final line could have been motivated out of humility, but perhaps it was rooted in irresponsibility. "Treat me as one of your hired servants." There is something very comfortable about that. A hired servant does not have to make responsible decisions. A hired servant is told what to do; whereas, a son is expected to make responsible decisions and to live up to these decisions.

What a relief in so many ways to be a hired servant! Why, you don't even have to love the father to be a hired servant. And you can punch in each day on the time clock for hired servants when you come to work and punch out as you leave, and when you leave at the end of the hired servant's work day, you can take not only your body, but your heart with you away from the father.

As a hired servant I guess you could even quit working for this father and go to work for some other man. You might even get better wages working elsewhere!

There is something within each of us that makes us want to be hired servants of God. Oh, don't get me wrong. We talk a great deal about being His children, but we often live before Him like hired servants.

Maybe no other Christian is more guilty of the hired servant syndrome than a pastor. After all, isn't that what a pastor is – a hired servant? The laity are volunteer servants, but the pastor is a hired servant, especially when the annual budget is voted on!

It is so easy to develop a hired servant mentality and a hired servant attitude. But the Father does not want us to be hired servants. He wants us to be responsible sons and daughters. The father will never receive us as a hired servant. He will only receive us as a son or daughter. We have never sinned against this Father as his hired servants. All of our sins have been committed against him as his sons and daughters. Doesn't the father in Luke's parable say at the end of the story, *For this my son* was *dead, and is alive again...?* (Luke 15:24a).

My son, the father said. This greatest of all stories is not a story about a man and his servant, but about a father and his son. This is not a story about hours and wages; it is a story about love and responsibility.

Hopefully, the boy in this story became a responsible son. The story concludes too early to tell us whether he did, but certainly it implies that he became a responsible son. I believe he became a responsible son for three reasons: because of something he discovered in the far country and because of two things he discovered upon his return home.

In the far country he discovered that he had left at home the one person in all the world who truly loved him. He left home to live for himself, only to discover that living for one's self leads to loneliness. He left home to find happiness, only to discover that his greatest moments of happiness had been spent in the past with one whom he called "Dad." He left home only to discover that home had not left him, for he had left at home the only person in this world who really loved him.

Now he did not know if this person still loved him. Remember, he had sinned and sinned greatly against this person. He had broken his father's heart. Which brings us to the first of two things he discovered upon returning home: not only did his father still love him, but he still loved him as a son.

Before the boy got all the way home, while he was yet at a great distance, his father saw him. *His father saw him.* That is another great phrase in the story. Neighbors who lived nearby might have seen just another destitute youth, or an alcoholic, or a beggar, or a drug addict, or a young man with AIDS, or whatever our sins do to our lives, but his father saw him.

And his father ran. Of course, you know the reason the man ran. He ran to welcome a hired servant back. And when he reached the youth, he threw his arms around him and embraced him, because that is what you do with hired servants when they return to work.

Turning to servants standing nearby, his father said, "Go get a robe, and put that robe on this hired servant. And get a ring and put it on the finger of this hired servant. And go bring shoes, for we can't have a barefooted hired servant. And one of you kill the fattened calf and prepare for a party, for a hired servant has come back to work."

Is that the way the story reads? Not quite! Instead, the words that are spoken from the father's mouth and heart are these: "Go bring a robe and be sure it is the best robe. Go bring a family ring from my own dresser. Go bring shoes. And kill the fattened calf and invite all the people in the village to come to a celebration because my son is home."

So when the boy came home, he discovered the father not only still loved him, but he still loved him as a son.

The boy also discovered when he returned home an incredible thing

39

he never knew in the far country: The father had suffered more than the son when the boy was away. I don't mean to make light of the young man's suffering, for he had suffered tremendously. He had gone without food, without friends, without money, without adequate clothing and without shelter, but the father had suffered even more because the boy was absent from home. When the old man threw his arms around the boy to embrace him on the road, if the boy had noticed the old man's hands, he would have seen scars in the hands resembling nail prints. As though someone had nailed "the old man" to a cross!

The old man had already suffered enough, so I am glad the son never actually said to his father, "Treat me as one of your hired servants." The boy had planned to say those words. They were to be the very last line in the speech he had rehearsed so well. But just before he could speak that last line to the father, his father interrupted the boy with the words to the servants. "Bring quickly the best robe, and put it on him…"

That is a touch of mercy in the story which most of us may have overlooked – the father never heard his son say, "Treat me as one of your hired servants." That might have been too much for the father's heart to bear. The father never wanted the boy to be a hired servant. He longed for the boy to be a responsible son. Remember, this is a story about a relationship.

The late J. Wallace Hamilton in one of his sermons told of a father who drove his son to a railroad station to put the boy on a train that would take the boy to a college far from home. It was the boy's first time to leave home. The father stood there beside the train for a long time just looking at the boy, wanting to say so many things to his son, but finally saying one thing which was more than enough, "Bill, never forget who you are."

I don't believe it can be expressed any better than that, so I lift up those words to every son and daughter of God. Never forget who you are!

CHAPTER SIX
The Robe
Luke 15:22a

A Hindu, after reading the story of The Prodigal Son for the first time, said, "This young man must have known me, for he has told my story." I wonder if this might be your story, too. I wonder if you might be this young man. Your first reaction to such a suggestion might be, "There is no way I am this young man. For one thing, I have never been so hungry I craved pig's food!"

But there are other ways to be broken other than economically. The spirit can be as bankrupt as the wallet. I have known at least as many people ruined by success as by failure. Even history confirms such truth. Alexander the Great, finding no more nations to defeat, died of depression at age thirty- three. The poet Lord Byron was dead of despair and grief at thirty-six. Voltaire spoke of the dark depths of his soul at the very time the people of Paris were cheering for him and calling his name.

No success in this world can make one happy. Tamerlane conquered almost half of his world, but he could not control his own craving spirit. So I am wondering if the boy in Jesus' story might be you.

When I was in high school, I heard for the first time the great poem *Invictus* by William Earnest Henley.

Out of the night that covers me,

Black as the pit from pole to pole,

I thank whatever gods may be

For my unconquerable soul.

That is the way Invictus begins, and it ends with these "unconquerable" words:

I am the master of my fate;

I am the captain of my soul.

Now that is the kind of man I am going to be I said to myself. But I did not know the whole story of Henley's life then, and my English teacher did not tell us the whole story. Perhaps she didn't know all the story – didn't know that Henley took his own life. That sometimes happens to men who are masters of their fate and captains of their soul.

The prodigal son in the far country was much like Henley. He thought he was the master of his own fate and the captain of his own soul. He didn't need anybody. He especially didn't need his father whom he thought was out-of-date and out-of-style until… Until he might have been within an hour of suicide himself. Until he uttered the remarkable line in the parable that caught him off guard: "I will leave here, and I will return to my father."

And I can't help wondering if you might be this boy. You, running as well as walking, to the far country. Wanting to get to the far-away land as quickly as you can. Running. But running with a haunting fear you can never completely shake. Like the poet Percy Shelley, who often dreamed of a strange masked enemy who would suddenly appear at the very moment Shelley won a great victory, seizing the reward of that victory and fleeing with the trophy.

One day in a dream Shelley stood at the wedding altar to marry the love of his life, when suddenly, the masked enemy appeared. Only this time, Shelley managed to grab him, ripped off the enemy's mask, and was overwhelmingly astonished to be looking at himself.

Could the boy in the far country possibly be you? Successful. Maybe highly successful, but empty. Like a line in a country song: "I would give all my tomorrows for just one yesterday." Successful, yet empty. Like lines in a Neil Diamond song:

And I am lost, and I can't even say why, leaving me lonely still....

But I've got an emptiness deep inside, and I've tried, but it won't let me go.

I believe an American president during my lifetime was empty. The most famous man in the world, but empty. The only reason I can offer for this feeling is simply that a preacher, if he is to communicate, has to be able to read faces, and I saw emptiness in his face.

The boy in the faraway land finally acknowledged his own emptiness with three words that said it all. *I have sinned.*

Sin is a word we are afraid to use or ashamed to use. Jim Bakker entitled his book about the shameful part of his life, *I Was Wrong*. Wrong is a mild word compared to the shocking word sinned. But there is no true forgiveness until we use the shocking word sinned. Forgiveness begins with, "I have sinned."

So the boy heads home. And after the long journey – and it was long because, remember, he had been in the far country – as he nears his home something happens that goes far beyond answering his deepest prayers and impossible dreams. Seeing him on the road, his father runs to meet him, not with justice, but with grace.

Theologians will tell you grace is unearned. But grace is more than unearned. It is also unexpected. In his wildest dreams and hopes the prodigal never imagined his father would run to him with grace and still call him son.

Yet his father's first word to him is *son*. The boy expects to hear sinner, but instead he hears *son*. The boy distinctly heard *son*. How could he not hear it? In all the dictionaries in this world and in all the titles of eternity, the boy knew the word son was the word he would never hear again from his father's lips. So how could he not hear it?

I said that forgiveness begins with I have sinned. It doesn't. My statement was only true of the human initiative in forgiveness. Forgiveness really begins with the divine initiative, which is "son."

There are many tangible signs of God's grace in this old story. But in the remainder of this sermon I want to submit one sign as the symbolic word of all the grace. The robe. The robe the father instructed a servant to bring to put on his son. We don't buy this garment. It is a gift. The only way to possess it is to accept it as a gift.

When King David of Israel wanted to offer an animal sacrifice to God on a day when he was not in Jerusalem but in the open country, he went to a farmer and said, "I want to buy wood in order to build an altar so I can make an offering to God." But the farmer said, "Oh no, my King, you do not need to buy wood or even oxen from me for your sacrifice. I will be honored to give them to you." David replied, "No! I want to pay you for them, for I will not offer to God that which cost me nothing." So David paid fifty shekels of silver. (This story is from 2 Samuel 24:20-24.)

I will not offer to God that which cost me nothing. They are noble words. Honorable words. Admirable. On those terms, however, David never would have worn the prodigal's robe. If we try to buy it at any price, even the price of the national debt, we will never be clothed in it. It is not for sale at any price. It is the robe of grace. It costs us nothing. Zero!

When the boy left for the far country, he had no intention of returning home. Since his father knew the boy's intentions, this must have crushed the father. Surely you could read the hurt in the father's face, except this boy – this selfish boy – had not really looked into his father's face. At least, he never looked his dad full in the face. This boy, in looking at faces, spent most of his time looking in a mirror.

If the boy had not run out of money in the far country, he might never have gone home. Which means his running out of money was grace. Let us remember that when finding ourselves burdened down. Some burdens are full of grace. They drive us to God!

My deep feeling, however, is that the boy would have gone back home even if he had not run out of money. It might have taken longer, for it probably takes a rich man longer to admit he is empty than it takes a poor man.

There is an old myth about the god of the sea in search of a man. The man escaped from the sea just in time to elude the grasp of the sea god. But as the man raced up the shore, a small wave was thrown in his heart. A smile then came upon the sea god's face, and he said, "The man will return to me; the sea is in his heart. He will be lonely and restless until he returns." Even so, I believe the Father put home, like a small wave, in his son's heart. Grace.

To accept the gift of the robe and to wear it means you are not returning home to be a servant or a second-hand citizen, but as a son or daughter. You are not coming back on probation. Not even for a day. Instead, you return home with all the rights and privileges of sonship.

This is not pardon. This is grace. Do you know the difference? If you are a criminal on death row, the governor has the authority to pardon you. In some of our states all it takes is a letter. In other states all it takes is a word. That is pardon.

Grace would be when the governor dies in your place. The New Testament knows nothing of forgiveness only by pardon. The forgiveness it knows is that of an innocent and sinless man nailed to a tree!

The robe is a gift. "Bring quickly the best robe, and put it on him…" The "best" robe. Wouldn't that be the father's robe? At least one translation – the New English Bible – thinks so: *"Quick! Fetch a robe, my best one, and put it on him…"* (Luke 25:22a NEB). The Father's best robe. What a gift.

Harry Emerson Fosdick told of a conversation with his father on the day Harry left home for college. On that day Harry gave his father the house key saying he would not be needing it. But his father gave the key back to Harry saying, "My boy, you keep the key and let it be a symbol as long as you live that you can come home anytime from anywhere and come in without knocking." Fosdick cherished those words the rest of his life.

Anytime. From anywhere. Would that include the far country? Sure. There is a best robe for you at your Father's home.

In January 1997 I saw an advertisement for a new book. The author was Bill Hybels. The title was *The God You're Looking For*. I have no interest in the book. Perhaps I should have, because it is written by a very successful and genuine pastor, so he probably shared some words in his book I need to know. But I am not interested in the God I am looking for. What interests me is the God who is looking for me. The Father who stands on the front porch of the old home-place day after day, watching and waiting for the return of his son from the far country. The seeking God. The running God. The God of grace. The God who can make my heart tremble forever.

I am not sure about the greatest moment as a father in relation to my youngest son, John Mark, but I know one of those moments. It came on June 24, 1996. Here is the background. John Mark graduated from law school in the spring of 1995. He took the Maryland state bar exam in the fall. It wasn't an easy exam, because a lot of students in his law school class failed, including the class president and the son of one of Maryland's most famous attorneys. But John Mark passed.

In that December, John Mark was sworn in as a member of the Maryland state bar. Then he waited to get a job as a lawyer. He did get a job in Howard County as a glorified law clerk, meaning he was more than a law clerk but less than an attorney. There is nothing wrong with being a law clerk, but my son did not go to law school to be a law clerk. Ever since his sophomore year in high school, being a lawyer was his dream, and he hitched himself to that star. He especially desired to be a prosecuting attorney.

The following spring John Mark learned he would lose his Howard County job that June. This was not because the county did not want to keep him. It was because the funding for the law clerk plus job would end then. This meant he not only would not have a job in the legal field, but he would have no job at all. And guess what was scheduled in his life on July 6, eight days after he would lose his job. His wedding. Talk about timing!

John Mark was not a happy camper. Saying he was down in the dumps would be far too mild. The truth is, I had never seen him so low in all his life.

It was not an easy time for young, hope-to-be-lawyers in Maryland. More than half of his law school's graduating class had not found a job as a lawyer. The young man who sat beside John Mark during the swearing in of the state bar took his own life because he could not find work as a lawyer. My son had not fallen that far, but he was really hurting, and because he hurt so much, his mother and I hurt also. To hurt for him and with him were our only resources.

Then on June 24, 1996, four days before John Mark was to lose his job and twelve days before his wedding, I received a telephone call at our home from John Mark. He called to tell me that he had gotten a job as the assistant state's attorney in Kent County, Maryland. He was to begin work after the honeymoon. This meant he would be a prosecuting attorney. His dream had come true.

After I hung up the phone, I went down the hall to another room where my wife Patsy was seated on the floor trying to put some books and magazines in some kind of order. I told her the wonderful news. She stood up and we embraced. And then we danced. Yes, we danced. We danced to words and to music that were neither sung nor played, but we heard music. Grace and joy have music all their own. So we danced. And danced. And danced… It is the most remembered and cherished dance of my life.

The father of the prodigal son danced at the party in honor of his son's home-coming. And for his attire at the dance he was not wearing his best robe. Because he had given his best robe to his son.

And his son wore it proudly but with the greatest humility. As though he knew it was the robe of grace…

CHAPTER SEVEN

The Fattened Calf
Luke 15:23a

Each time I finish writing a new sermon about the prodigal son, I tell myself that surely this will be my last sermon on the story. I tell myself that surely this parable will never speak to me again. I have exhausted it, or it is has exhausted me. There is no more new in it, I tell myself. I have overlooked nothing in it I am certain.

But then my eyes see something I overlooked. My heart trembles with a thought it had not felt: *the* fattened *calf.* As much as I like steak, I don't know how I missed "the fattened calf."

Bring the fattened calf and kill it. Let us look at the definite article *the* in the verse. Since I majored in Greek as well as theology at seminary, I should not have overlooked "the." I should have remembered that in Greek – the language of the New Testament – the definite article is never used unless it is describing "the special one," or "the unique one" or "the greatest one."

For years I was aware of the use of the definite article in Jesus' conversation with Nicodemus in the encounter that led to John 3:16. In this encounter Jesus said to Nicodemus, "Are you *the* teacher of Israel, yet you don't understand how one can be born again?" In that context when Jesus used *the* before "teacher," he was acknowledging that Nicodemus was recognized as the greatest teacher in Israel. The New English Bible even translates Jesus' question to Nicodemus, "What! Is this famous teacher of Israel ignorant of such things?" (John 3:10 NEB). The New International Version translates, "You are Israel's teacher...."

But for years I overlooked the fattened calf. It stands in great contrast to Jesus' use of the indefinite article with two other instructions to the father's servants. They are told to bring for his son *a* ring, and *a* pair of sandals, but they are clearly told to kill *the* fattened calf.

You may wonder why I make such a big deal over a small matter or what difference it could possibly make. It makes an enormous difference. It makes the difference called hope and the difference called grace.

There was hope where there was no reason to hope, for this had been no little selfish fling on the part of the prodigal. It was a total and complete rejection of his past, his home, and most of all, his father. He wanted to go as far away from his past as he could. He didn't just want to get far away in distance. He wanted to get far away in memory. He wanted to forget the past, including his dad. He wanted to get far enough away to be a different kind of person in every kind of way. He wanted to be in full control of his choices and call all the shots. He went to a far country. So far that he would never go back. So far he would not even remember how to get back.

Try placing yourself in this father's place. If you are a father, as I am, that is easy. As his father, knowing your son's attitude and mind-set and heart-bent when he left, how much hope would you have that your son would come home?

You might ask yourself, "Which one of the commandments I taught him is he breaking tonight? Did he really mean it when he said he could never have my kind of faith and would not want it even if he could? He lived by reason and not by faith. He said he had no belief in prayer, so what are the chances he is praying tonight?" Sounds hopeless to me.

Place yourself in this father's place. Your son has ruined your life and it hurts. But do you know what hurts more? That he is ruining his own life.

He probably thinks he is having fun right now, but he is not having joy. He probably thinks he is really being loved tonight, but he is only being gratified. He may really think he is living, but he is only existing. He's treading water. He may be laughing today, and he probably would never believe this, but I want him to laugh. I just want him to know the laughter of true love and not the laughter of selfish sin.

Sons away from home. My, how they bring grief to us. O. Henry, who wrote many marvelous stories, in one of those stories told about a young man who moved from a little village to a great city. In the village the young man was reared in a good home by loving parents, and he was taught in a good school where teachers cared about him as a student, and even more, as a person. But in the city he became a criminal. He never was caught in a crime, but crime was more and more becoming his vocation.

One day, just after committing a crime, he saw in the city a young lady he had known and loved in the little village. She did not see him. She was just as fresh and sweet and innocent and pure as she had been. He looked at her, and then he looked at himself, and he leaned his head against a lamppost and said, "God, how I hate myself." [9]

I think the prodigal in the far country came to the place where he hated himself. He ended up in a pig's pen craving pig's food. If that doesn't make one hate himself, I don't know what can.

O. Henry's story was fiction, but the point of it is reality. The reality of life in the far country.

Now, here is a story that is true. A drunk bum was brought to Bellevue Hospital from the Bowery in New York City. He was a charity case, one among hundreds.

His throat was slashed from a fall, so a doctor was called in to sew up the wound. The doctor used black sewing thread for, after all, this man was from the Bowery. This treatment was not enough to bring healing because the man died three days later.

At the morgue they found in his ragged, dirty coat all the possessions he had left except for the clothing on his body. In one of the two pockets of the coat they found thirty-eight cents. In the other pocket they found a scrap of paper with five words on it: "Dear friends and gentle hearts." The words almost sounded like a song.

It turns out they were the words of a song, and the derelict had written the song. He also had written more than 200 other songs. Among them were "Oh! Susanna!" "Beautiful Dreamer," "Jeanie with the Light Brown Hair," "Old Folks at Home," and "My Old Kentucky Home."

It seems Stephen Foster got too far away from that old Kentucky home. He had written songs that made the whole world sing, but there was no song in his own heart. The laughter in his last days was only the laughter of the far country. And it was an empty laughter, hollow and lonely. [10]

Such were the fears of the father in Luke's parable. He knew the far country would destroy his son in a thousand ways. His boy would die hating himself in that lonely land. All hope was gone.

Then why "the fattened calf"? The fattened calf is the symbol of hope. Without hope, our lives become meaningless. In the play, South Pacific, Mary Martin sang, "I'm stuck like a dope with thing called hope, and I can't get it out of my mind."

Hope is a wonderful thing to be stuck with, and the father in the parable was stuck with it. If not, then why the fattened calf? This father has never lost hope. Not with the fattened calf in his barn.

Even when death comes – and it will come to all of us – there is hope. In "the land beyond the river" there is the fattened calf. And, more than that, in death's far country there is the Lamb who was slain by his own free will to save us from hopelessness.

A congregation never gathers for worship but that someone in the crowd has lost hope. A book is never read but that some readers have lost hope. If you have lost hope, I want you to know that the swallows will come back to Capistrano. You will laugh again. You will love and be loved. If not, why the fattened calf? The fattened calf brings hope.

But the calf is also a symbol of something more than hope. It is a symbol of the Father's grace. Think of it this way. If I, a human father, had a son in the far country, and I did not know how horrible his life might be and how tragic his choices in the land far away, I would want to believe I would never lose hope for his homecoming. I would like to feel that in my barn or in my fields, the fattened calf would always be ready for a party in honor of my son who would come home. Let that be my hope.

But it could be a vain hope. Because my knowledge is limited. I recall a great deal of my past, even more of my present, but absolutely nothing of my future. I don't know if my son will come home. At best, my knowledge is limited.

The great parable, however, is not about a human father. It is about a divine Father who knows everything. Past. Present. Future. You may think it is hard not knowing what is going on in the life of your son. Do you think it would be easier if you knew? Do you think it would be easier to know that one month from today they are going to kill your only begotten son? They will strip him, beat him, curse him, humiliate him, and crucify him between two criminals. Would that lift some of the weight of concern?

The son in the story, of course, is not the divine son. He is a human son. Like you and me. Sinner. Selfish. Unloving. Pleasure seeker. Not caring about anyone but ourselves. Not even caring if the Old Man back home is dead or alive.

But the divine father knew the conclusion of the far country story. His son hungry to almost starvation. Craving pig's food. Have you ever been so hungry you stole food from pigs? If you had a son who was a long way from home and stealing food from pigs, does knowing this hurt less than not knowing?

I am grateful that this father, in seeing the future, saw beyond the pigpen. He saw his son returning home.

Actually, it was the Father's grace that got the boy home. Grace came in the form of an economic depression, loss of all money, loss of friends, feeding pigs, emptiness and hopelessness. That was all grace, because grace is that which gets you home.

Seeing his son on the road as the young man approaches home, he runs to him and embraces him. He listens to his son's confession of sin, but he interrupts the confession, which is to say he let his son confess some of his sin but not all of it. He has heard enough. He stops the boy when the boy expresses his concern about how much (or how little) his father might love him now.

The father says: "Let me tell you something, Son. I could not love you less if I were to try. You are my son. You will always be my son, and I will always love you with all my heart."

"One of you servants bring *a* family ring for my son and another bring *a* pair of shoes for my son. And, you there, go kill *the* fattened calf…"

Hope. How precious it is. Grace. How amazing it is.

CHAPTER EIGHT

The Party

Luke 15:23b

Karl A. Olsson in his book, *Come to the Party*, said there are four groups of Christians in this world. I suppose some in these groups are not Christians, but they think they are. These four groups are distinguished from each other by their attitude toward "The Party."

The first group doesn't even know there is a party going on, at least not in the kingdom of God. In the far country maybe. That's why the prodigal son left home for the far country where he could party.

There are some people who never laugh in church. Even if I say something in a sermon that is so funny most of the people almost roll in the aisles in laughter, these people will not laugh. Well, perhaps once every ten or so years they laugh a little. They go, "Ha. Ha." But that's the extent of it.

I'm not advocating that Christians should always be smiling in good times and bad times. Someone said, "If you smile when everything goes wrong, you're either a nitwit or a repairman." Come to think of it, the repairman always shows up at my door smiling.

But we do owe it to our world, to God's world, to let people know there is laughter in the kingdom of God. There is laughter within the walls of the church. Millions of people don't know that. Theodore F. Adams tells of a little boy who prayed, "Lord, help me to be perfect, but not too perfect because then you don't have any fun."

This reminds me of another little boy who, when asked to describe Christians, said, "Christians are mild, weak, quiet people who never fight or talk back." Then he added, "Daddy is a Christian, but Mother isn't." Isn't that precious?

Lavonn Brown said that when he was thinking of becoming a Christian, he believed that you had to make a list of ten things you like to do and stop doing them. Then you must make a list of ten things you don't like to do and start doing them. I wonder how many Christians believe that?

More than half a century ago Peter Marshall in his usual eloquence reminded us that God is the God of our laughter as well as the God of our prayers. God is the God of our singing as well as the God of our tears. Marshall went on to say that God is very much at home in the play of his children, for He loves to hear us laugh.

Do you agree? Do you believe the Man out of Nazareth laughed? Jesus may have laughed more than any other man who has ever lived. I am serious. Serious about, of all things, his laughter.

Don't ever try to take Jesus' sorrows away from me. In the depths of my life I need to identify with his sorrows in order to cope. But don't ever attempt to take away his laughter either. I need his laughter in order to enjoy and in order to be free and, even more, in order to be me.

Do you know God has a fun side? Do you know the laughing Jesus? Do you know there is a party going on in the great kingdom of God?

Charles Spurgeon, the revered English preacher, said it is unfortunate that the calendar of the church only has a few days marked as festival days. I think that is quite true. Too many Christians are not aware of the partying God.

C. S. Lewis, the great intellect who gave up his agnosticism for Christianity, said he felt in the moment of his conversion that he was the most dejected convert in all of England, and do you know why? Because he thought he would never have fun again. He did not know about the party.

The second group of Christians does know there is a party going on in the kingdom of God. But they do not know they have been invited to the party. The Roman soldier who approached Jesus to ask him to heal a servant, saying to Jesus, "I know I am so unworthy that you would never enter my home," did not realize that Jesus was willing to enter his home. The soldier did not know the party was for him.

There was a leper in the Scriptures who had no idea the party was for him. When he approached Jesus to beg Jesus to heal him, he began to shout, "Unclean! Unclean!" The Law required this, for lepers were not permitted to get too close to healthy people. In other words, he hoped for healing by Jesus' voice and not by touch of hand, for this man knew Jesus would never touch him. But, in what for me is one of the most inspirational moments in the Bible, Jesus reached out and touched him as he healed him. The leper must have been bewildered by this touch.

Most of us living in the United States find it difficult to identify with lepers, because we are not lepers ourselves, and we really don't know any lepers. But in our own time and place, at last, we have a metaphor in our society to understand the fear of leprosy, *AIDS*. This man with *AIDS* could not believe Jesus would ever touch him. He had no awareness that he was invited to the party.

The centurion. The leper. And the list goes on. Matthew, the despised tax collector. The thief on the cross. The woman at the well. Simon Peter, falling to his knees before Jesus, exclaiming, "Lord, depart from me, for I am a great sinner." Saul of Tarsus about noon on the road to Damascus. And don't omit John Newton, former captain of a slave ship, who gave to Christianity the everlasting hymn, "Amazing Grace." For Newton, the most amazing thing about God's grace is that it included him. He was invited to the party!

Yet there are people reading this sermon who do not believe the amazing grace includes grace for them. Some past sin or sins keep them from the door to the party. They are not among the chosen.

Pieces

But every one of us is among the chosen! You are a child of God the Father, and all God's children have been invited. You are one of the sinners for whom God the Son gave his life. That is why the great verse, John 3:16, had the great word *whosoever*.

> For God so loved the world, that he gave his only begotten Son, that whosoever believeth in him should not perish, but have everlasting life." (KJV)

And God the Holy Spirit delivers the invitation to the party to your own heart. In other words, God himself comes. He does not send messenger boys. This invitation comes straight from God, and the announcement is written in the very blood of the Son of God. Never say that you are not among the chosen.

In our parable the younger son went to live in the far country. This country had another name. It was the Sin country. That is why the son went to the far country, and that is what he did when he got there. He sinned. Day after day. Sin after sin.

But a day came in the far country when finally sin paid its wage. Sin always has its wage. In our sin we start off thinking that sin is our slave. It is always under our control. But the day finally comes in Sin's far country when you hit rock bottom, and you realize sin has lied to you all along. The truth is that sin is the master. We are sin's slave. Sin is not under our control. It never has been. Sin controls us. It dominates our hearts.

At the depths of his slavery to sin, the youth makes a decision to return home and beg his father to employ him. He would ask to be a mere employee. In the Greek language there are two words for "employee." One means "a permanent employee" with a secure job, benefits, tenure, etc. The second word means "day laborer." In Jesus' story the word is "day laborer." It was the very best he could hope for. One thing he knew for sure: The party was not for him.

The third of the four groups of people knows there is a party going on in the kingdom of God and they even know they have been invited, but they believe they have been invited because of something they will bring to the party. Money. Gifts. Success. Something accomplished. Something achieved. Something possessed. Something earned – but something.

I think the prodigal son felt he needed to offer his father something. Perhaps his something was the money he would earn as a day laborer. Had his father let him continue with his spiel there on the road at his homecoming, he would have told his father that from his earnings as a day laborer he would be willing to pay his father for the money he wasted in the far country. He knows now that the money he wasted was not his money but his father's.

So I think the payback approach might have been his when he returned from the far country. Many people use the payback approach when confronting God. Reimbursing the Father as if one could reimburse sin! Pretending and presuming that Calvary never happened!

Invited to the party because the host wants something you will bring. How often we fall in that trap. But this is a grace party, and at a grace party there is nothing we can bring and offer the host because Jesus paid it all. Elvina M. Hall said it eloquently.

> Jesus paid it all,
> All to him I owe;
> Sin had left a crimson stain,
> He wash'd it white as snow.

This was a grace party, and perhaps the greatest evidence of the grace was the father running down the road to embrace his son. This greatest of gentlemen runs.

Let's pretend the boy in the parable returned home when he was twenty, and ten years have passed so he is now thirty. And let's give this thirty-year-old a name. Let's just give him my name, Lewis. And let's pretend a new friend of mine who is also about thirty asks me this question.

"Lewis, I am sure you never saw your father run, did you?"

"Yes, to tell you the truth, once I saw him run. Only once."

"It must have been something big, something incredibly big, to make him run, Lewis."

"Yes, it was. You didn't know me ten years ago, and I am ashamed to tell you that, had you known me then, you would have had no respect for me. Because I rejected my father. And it was not because he had failed me in some big way. It was I who failed him. I chose to fail him. I rejected him. I told him one day that I did not want to wait around until he died to get my part of his inheritance. I said I wanted my portion then so I could go live in a far country. In a way, he surprised me by giving it to me. I realize now he had the wisdom to know that if my heart was in the far country, it didn't mean much just to have my body at home. So Dad gave me the money. A lot of money. And I went to that far country, and I spent every last dollar of it on sin and my own selfishness.

"A day came in the far country when I was broke. Broke in about every way a man can be broke. I lost all hope. In those depths life played a strange paradox. My body was in the far country, but my heart was home. So I started home. I determined that when I confronted Dad at home, I would ask him if he would employ me as a day laborer. It was all I could hope for and far more than I deserved. It was a long journey, so I had a lot of time to think and reflect, mostly about my foolishness. Finally, I reached the place on the road where I got my first glimpse of home even though I was still a distance away. I saw the fields of home and the big house on the hill. The house I knew I would never enter again, for day laborers are not allowed to enter.

"Suddenly I saw a man running. Running toward me. I wondered who was running, and then I realized it was Dad. I was terrified. Was he running to beat me, to kill me, to condemn me, to put a curse on me? It was the greatest fear I have ever known. More frightening even than the famine and hard times in the far country. But he just kept on running. When he reached me, he threw open his arms – not to hit me, but to embrace me – and he said to me, 'Son, I love you so very much. I am so glad you are home.' You asked me if I ever saw my father run. Yes, that one time."

You see, it was a grace party. What gifts or honors did this boy bring to the party? None. The only thing he had to bring was the rags he wore. No one of us ever brings more than rags to the grace party. The words of the prophet Isaiah are brutally honest and brutally accurate: *"All of us have become like one who is unclean, and all our righteous acts are like filthy rags"* (Isaiah 64:6).

Finally, there is a fourth group in the story about the party. Those in this group know there is a party taking place in the kingdom of God, and they know they have been invited. Furthermore, they know their invitation to the party is not because the host desires something from them, because all they have are filthy rags. But they show up at the door of the party anyway. They go in and enjoy the sheer gift of grace.

Some time ago I read a line in a book of fiction that described what sin is. It staggered my mind and spoke deeply to my heart, because no book of theology I have read – and I have read many – gives anything close to this line as a definition of sin: "That is what sin really is. You know – not *being full of joy*."[11]

You have been invited to the Party. Accept the invitation and show up. Because if you don't, you will never be full of joy.

CHAPTER NINE

At the Depth of Lost
Luke 15:25-32

At the depth of lost. What horrible sin lies at the deepest level of one's separation from God? Is it murder or lying or idolatry? Is it fornication or rape or mental cruelty? Or, to name some of the sins of the heart, is it covetousness or lust?

At the depth of lost there are none of these, not even lust. Instead, at the deepest level of one's separation from God there are two traits which are found in the elder son in Jesus' parable about the father and his two sons. The two traits are that he felt he had done nothing for which to apologize, and he felt that he had nothing for which to be thankful.

In my opinion there is no other person in the Bible – neither a real person nor a character in a parable – who is as lost as this elder son. You might want to challenge that, knowing that this son has spent the days of his years either in his father's house or on his father's land serving his father and knowing that no other person has been as obedient and as responsible to duty in the service of his father as he. His father, of course, is God.

How unlike his younger brother. The younger brother had requested his share of the inheritance from his father early. He wanted it before his father died. And when his father gave this share to him, he went to live in a far country, which means he went as far away from his father as he could possibly go. There he wallowed in some of the gross sins mentioned in the outset of this sermon. But the son in sin's far country was not as lost as the son who stayed home and served his father. The boy who stayed home lived day by day with those two traits that are at the depth of being lost: nothing for which to apologize and nothing for which to be thankful.

Let us consider these two traits. First, he felt he had done nothing that needed apology. Absolutely nothing at all!

That is certainly not the mind-set of the younger son because one day in the far country when he found himself in the gutter – the gutter was actually a better place than where he was which was in the pigpen – he said, "I have sinned." After that, he says something else. He says, "I no longer deserve to be called my father's son." And after that, he says even more. "I am going home to Dad and see if he will allow me to be one of his employees for the rest of my life, for I am no longer worthy to be his son. I have sinned. I have hit rock bottom, and it is all my fault. I have no one to blame but me. This was my doing. I am the one who chose to sin."

So in this familiar story, as you know, the boy goes home and tells his father the truth, the truth of his sin. His was a lifestyle of such depravity and disgrace that he no longer deserves to be called his father's son. But when he tells his father this, the first word out of his father's mouth is, "Son." And his father's next words are, "I love you, and I forgive you, and you will always be my son. I am so glad you are home, Son."

And right then and there, by giving some orders to his many servants, he gives his son a new suit – well maybe, first he gives him a bath because the boy still smells like the pigsty – to replace the rags he wears. He also gives him a ring for his hand – probably a sign of sonship – and shoes for his bare feet.

His father next orders a servant to slaughter the fattest calf he owns and to prepare for a banquet. He sends servants out to invite the whole community to the banquet to celebrate with him and rejoice with him because his son who was so lost – so lost it was as if he were dead – is home.

At the start of the celebration, the father says, "Let there be music and dancing."

And so there is music and there is dancing; in fact, the music and the hand clapping and the foot stomping are so loud the older son working in his father's fields hears all the noise of the party.

He starts walking toward the house to see what is going on. Near the house, he confronts a servant and says to him, "What is going on?" The servant answers with excitement and enthusiasm, "Good news! Your brother is home, and your father is having a party in his honor. Hurry on to the house, for surely your father wants you at this celebration."

But he doesn't go in because he is angry. So his father, hearing about his anger, goes out to find him. This Father always seeks us. We as the sinners should seek him, but the sinless Father seeks us.

Finding him, the father says to him "What are you doing out here, for a servant just told me that you know your brother is home? Why aren't you already in the house celebrating and rejoicing with the rest of us?"

His son answers harshly, "All the years of my life I have served you faithfully, and I have never broken even one of your commandments at any time, but you have never slaughtered even a small goat to have a party in my honor. Yet, the moment this, your son, comes home, he who has wasted your money on harlots, you order the fattened calf killed, and you have a party in his honor!"

The depth of lost. It is all there in those hot, angry words which say that he has never done anything to apologize for. "All the years of my life I have served you faithfully..." How can he say he has served his father faithfully when his heart is so full of everything absent from his father's heart, things like self-centeredness, jealousy, and unlove?

"Yet, the moment this, your son, comes home..." "Your son" – that is a strange wording. Shouldn't it be "my brother"? If my oldest son, Steven, is introducing my other two sons to you, he will not say, "I would like for you to meet my father's son, David, and my father's son, John Mark." I can't imagine him ever phrasing it that way. He will say instead, "I would like for you to meet my brothers, David and John Mark."

But this older boy in the parable can't even call his brother *brother*. In other words, he denies that he is his brother. If a father has two sons, and the older son denies his brother, I can't think of anything that could hurt the father's heart much more than that. The older son in Jesus' story tells his father that he has never broken any of his father's commandments. That's right. All he has broken is his father's heart!

"But when this son of yours who has wasted your money on harlots comes home…" Who told this older son that bit of information? His brother didn't. He hasn't even seen his younger brother since his brother returned home. His father didn't tell him and no servant told him. Where did he get the news that his brother had wasted his father's wealth on harlots?

Is he jealous? Does he wish he could have fulfilled his own desires with harlots, provided his father did not find out? I remember H. G. Wells' definition of "moral indignation." He called it "jealousy with a halo." But because the elder son had not actually committed such gross sin, he wants his brother punished with no forgiveness. His father's forgiveness of his younger son is the reason for the great anger of his older son, reminding me of a comment Samuel H. Miller once made. He said the Pharisees, and Jesus aimed his story about the elder son at the Pharisees, were frightened by Jesus' "promiscuous forgiveness."

But the fact is, both sons in the parable need just as much of the Father's forgiveness. Just as much. For in getting forgiveness we get all of it, or we get none of it. One cannot say, "I will give you so much forgiveness but nothing beyond that." If to this day in your life you have committed only one sin, and a little sin at that, Jesus still would have had to be crucified to atone for your one sin. That is why there is no such thing as a little sin.

Lord Byron said it so well in one of his poems:

> In men whom men condemn as ill
> I find so much of goodness still,

In men whom men pronounce divine

I find so much of sin and blot,

I do not dare to draw a line

Between the two where God has not.[12]

But so often we draw that line. We say, "Love stops here. Beyond this, my love will not go. This person deserves love, but this one does not." But that is not the way the Father in the parable loves. His love is unconditional, as is his forgiveness.

However, to know his forgiveness and to know eternal life, there is one great requirement. One must admit this need. One of the Watergate criminals, Jeb Magruder, gave his life to Christ after his crime and became a Christian minister. In this new role he was speaking at a banquet, and he began his speech saying, "The only reason I am able to stand here before you this evening is because someone forgave me."

But the elder son felt there was nothing he needed to apologize for. Nothing! At such a depth of being lost not even God can reach a person with His forgiveness. What possible difference could forgiveness make to a man who believes he has no need of it?

The second trait of the depth of lost in the life of the elder son is that he felt there was nothing that had ever happened in his life to be thankful for. If there was just one meaningful thing in his life which had been given to him as a gift, one thing he received he knew he had not earned, I believe he might have rejoiced that his wayward brother had come home. But there was nothing meaningful or beautiful or lovely or precious to him that in his own mind he had not earned. Nothing!

An old prayer said, "For all thy blessings, known and unknown, remembered and forgotten, we give Thee thanks." What a thoughtful and thankful prayer. But there is none of that spirit in the elder son. "Old Man, I have worked for you for years, never breaking any of your commandments, but you never gave me anything." That is his spirit.

The fact is, his father gave him everything. Every morning at breakfast he gave him something. "Good morning, Son." Son. Hear that word. Hear it as the hired servants heard it. They knew its meaning and its gift. Would they have traded places with him? Gladly and quickly.

"Join me in working in the fields today, Son." You fool, this is God talking, and he is calling you "Son." And do you know the greatest gift he has planned for you today while you are standing out here in the field pouting? He has planned for you to help your Dad welcome your brother home, Son. "Son, you are always with me, and all that I have is yours. It was right that we should make merry and be glad, for your brother was dead and is alive again, and was lost and is found" (Luke 15:31-32 NKJV).

How very much this elder son had to be thankful for, yet he felt there was nothing to be thankful for. How different is the attitude of the younger son when he comes home to the father he had betrayed with all his sins, only to be met with forgiveness of such magnitude that he would never forget it the rest of his life. The younger son knows he has everything to be thankful for, while the older son knows he has nothing for which to be thankful.

"For it is by grace you have been saved, through faith," Paul writes in Ephesians 2:8, *"and this* not *from yourselves, it is the gift of God...."* This tells us that even our faith is the gift of God. It does not mean that we have no choice in the matter because we do. But it does mean that even our capacity for faith is also a gift of His grace. And the compassionate appeal of the Holy Spirit, who speaks to our minds and hearts, if only we will listen, encouraging us to accept Jesus as Savior and Lord, is likewise a gift of the Father's grace. Ultimately it is the appeal of Calvary. What kind of man can hear of Calvary and still think he has nothing for which to give thanks?

In the beautiful novel, Cry, the Beloved Country, by the late Alan Paton, Stephen Kumalo's son is on trial for murder. Kumalo is a poor man, and not having the resources to help his son, he seeks the wisdom of a priest. The priest persuades a lawyer to help Kumalo's son, and this lawyer is one of the greatest in South Africa where Kumalo lives. The priest tells Kumalo the good news which is that the great lawyer will take the case *pro deo*.

Kumalo is very grateful to learn that the lawyer will take the case, and at the same time he is worried about what surely will be an enormous legal fee. He expresses his concern to the priest. The dialogue between the two of them is one of the most poignant moments in the award-winning novel.

"You may thank God that we have got this man.... He is a great man, and one of the greatest lawyers in South Africa, and one of the greatest friends of your people."

"I do thank God, and you too, father. But tell me. I have one anxiety, what will it cost? My little money is nearly exhausted."

"Did you not hear me say he would take the case pro deo? Ah yes, you have not heard of that before. It is Latin, and it means for God. So it will cost you nothing, or at least very little."

"He takes it for God?"

"That is what it meant in the old days of faith, though it has lost much of that meaning. But it still means that the case is taken for nothing."

Kimalo stammered. "I have never met such kindness," he said. He turned away his face, for he wept easily in those days.[13]

Pro deo. He takes it for God. But when it comes to our deepest need – atonement for our sins – only God can take it for God. And he did. At Calvary God took it for God. God, the Father, took it. There is a puny and ignorant theology that advocates that the Father God has a mean streak; that He is not loving like Jesus, and this is why He sent Jesus to the Cross to die for our sins.

But the Apostle Paul knew better. Paul penned the truth in his letter to the Church in Corinth, and this truth is full of grace: *"...God was in Christ reconciling the world to Himself..."* (2 Corinthians 5:19 NKJV). Thus the father in the parable gave his own life for his sons. Both sons.

What kind of man can stand at the foot of the Cross, the Father's Cross, and feel no need to apologize for anything and feel that there is nothing which ever happened in his life for which he owes thanks?

A man at the depth of lost...

CHAPTER TEN
God Had Three Sons
Luke 15:11-32

Most of the time we who preach the Gospel conclude the story of the prodigal son too soon. We tend to close the story when the younger son, the prodigal, repents and comes home where he receives his father's forgiveness.

The Father in the parable, of course, is God. But this is not just a story about God and his son. It is about God and his sons. There is more than one son in the story. There are even more than two. There are three sons. We are most familiar with the son who left home to sin. When he got away from the presence of his father, he didn't pretend to be anything except a sinner. Sinning was his lifestyle. He enjoyed sin! He found pleasure in it. To him sinning was the way to fun and happiness. He was without pretense. He was what he appeared to be, a fun-loving sinner. Away from his father's home he was completely free to choose what he wanted to do with his life. His free choice was to sin.

Many sinners in this world today fall in a similar category. They sin because it is the lifestyle they choose. They wouldn't have it any other way. Sin is their aim. Their goal. Their want. Their need. Their life. It is even their god.

It doesn't do any good to try to get them in the church because they have no desire to be in church. It is useless to talk to them about morals because morals to them are stupid. Something for the unsophisticated. The backward. The very old. So it is useless to confront them with their sins, because they know they are sinners and they don't want to change.

When such a person starts sinning, there is no awareness as to where his sin will lead. Years ago I read about drug peddlers in Thailand who wanted to smuggle drugs across the border from Thailand to Malaysia. They decided to do this by kidnapping babies or by purchasing babies from homes where parents were too poor to provide for their babies. They would murder these babies and cut open their little bodies to fill them with small bags of heroin. They would then hire women to carry these babies across the border under the pretense that the babies were asleep. When you read something like this, you say to yourself, "What kind of person would do this? Only a monster would do this!"

But actually anyone who has made sin his lifestyle is capable of it. Sin is one of those things that when you get it started, you seem unable to stop it. It seems to have only an accelerator and no brake. Perhaps it has brakes at first, but one's lifestyle wears out the brakes, while it never seems to run out of gas. It just goes on and on, faster and faster, bigger and bigger, until one day one of two things happens. You come to yourself, as did the prodigal in the far country, and you go home and ask forgiveness of your father, as he did. Or you surrender your life to sin that has become your god!

God had three sons. One left home to sin – to sin openly and without apology. At some point in Christian history he was labeled "the prodigal son."

But this old story also tells about a second son. He is the one who compels us to rearrange our list of cardinal sins, because we tend to put sins of passion at the top of our sin list; whereas, such things as jealousy, pride, and greed barely get on the list. We are more apt to call them "faults" than to call them "sins."

But Jesus played havoc with the world's sin list. He treated sins of passion with pity. Great pity. He never condoned such sin or made little of such sin, but when the passionate one repented and asked Jesus for forgiveness, Jesus responded with great mercy. For example, he said one day to a repentant harlot, "Your faith has saved you; go in peace" (Luke 7:50). But Jesus met the exclusive pride of some of the religious leaders with scorching wrath, terrible to behold, telling them prostitutes would get into the kingdom of God before they would. Self-righteousness almost always drew Jesus' greatest condemnation.

So in the parable we also confront the second sinful son. The one who stayed home to sin. The one whose self-righteousness is overwhelming. And my, how furious his self-righteousness was when he learned from a servant that his brother had come home and his father was having a party to celebrate his brother's homecoming. This older brother, when learning the reason for the party was to celebrate his brother's homecoming, could have said, "How glad I am, and how happy this must be for Dad."

But that was by no means his reaction. The truth is that he said absolutely nothing to the informing servant. At least the Scripture doesn't reveal any words he might have said. There was no need for words. His face said it all. His countenance revealed his thoughts. He just stood there in the field with his face burning with anger, jealousy, and even hatred. He would not go to the party.

Thus there are two prodigals in the story. One a prodigal in the far country. The other a prodigal at home. They were both separated from their father. One by passion and the other by pride.

To be fair to the older son, I must admit he deserved some praise. He was steadily industrious. On the day the story unfolds he has been in the fields working all day. He was dependable, conscientious and consistent. You could always count on him. Although he was not generous, he was just.

So wherein did he sin? He sinned because he never really appreciated his father's companionship. He seemed unaware of the daily bounty of home. He never realized that his opportunities were mostly by gift rather than by merit so that he complained most of the time instead of rejoicing.

His brother was now enjoying a feast of happiness and welcome, yet he had sat daily at his father's table. For his brother a spring of mercy had been struck from the rock of desolation, but for him a quiet river of grace had overflowed.

The irony is he seemed to think he deserved all this. That is the problem with self-righteousness. It leads one to think he deserves grace. *"Look! All these years I have been slaving* for *you and never disobeyed your orders,"* the older son in the field says to his father (Luke 15:29). What an extravagant claim! It is especially so when one realizes the Father to whom he is speaking is God.

How different is the claim of Paul. Writing to the church in Philippi he spoke of his own spiritual achievement with great humility: *"Not that I have already obtained all this, or have already been made perfect, but I press on to take hold of that for which Christ Jesus took hold of me* (Philippians 3:12). Many years after Paul encountered Jesus on the road to Damascus and gave his life to Jesus, Paul wrote, *"Christ Jesus came into the world to save sinners – of whom I am the worst"* (1 Timothy 1:15). Put that up against the son in the field saying to his father, "I never disobeyed your orders." Unless we live very close to Jesus we are always in danger of becoming a Pharisee, lost in our own self-worth.

Perhaps he even had a greater sin than his self-righteousness. Something going on in his life that even overshadowed his selfish pride. He was loveless. He never felt his brother's suffering in the far country, and he never shared his father's great grief.

It saddens me that when the story ends, the passionate sinner is in his father's house, but the prideful sinner is still outside in the field. It is extremely sad because no one shut him out. He shut himself out. He refused to go in. He was barred from home by his lovelessness.

And do you know what we call lovelessness? We call it a fault. We don't call it sin, but it is sin. So thus far there are two sons. The one who left home to sin and the one who stayed home to sin.

But there is also a third son of God in the story. He is not directly mentioned in the story, but because this story is a miniature of the Gospel, he is, for sure, part of the story. The third son is the son who left his Father's side to save both of his brothers.

He left his Father's side to save his brother in the far country who had wasted his life in "riotous living" because he knew that people need loving the most when they deserve it the least. And he left his Father's side to save his brother in the field so near to home, yet so far away, because he knew that the most pathetic of all men is the man who thinks he deserves his Father's love. The man who forgets – or maybe never knows – that love is the greatest gift.

It is the third son who redeems the story. This third son left home to save you because you, like me, are one of two kinds of sinners. We are either the one who strayed from home to sin, or we are the one who stayed home to sin. They both need the Father just as desperately, and that is why the third son left his heavenly home to bring us to the Father.

A story is told of a man standing at the top of a tall building, and as he looked down at the street below, he saw cars that looked the size of small toy cars and real people who looked like miniature people. As he stood there looking down at little cars and little people, he said to himself, "This must be the way the earth looks to God."

Of course, this is not the way the earth looks to God. Instead of viewing earth from the top of a tall building or seated on a star, He sees it from a cross where the view is not vertical but horizontal. For in Jesus God Himself came into our far country of sin or into our field of sin to give in love his holy life so that all of us, if only we will, can go home again.

So I thank God for a very special brother. His name is Jesus.

Sweetest note in seraph song,

Sweetest name on mortal tongue;

Sweetest carol ever sung,

Jesus, blessed Jesus.

-William Hunter

CHAPTER ELEVEN
East of Eden
Genesis 3:23-24

In the chapter which follows I have given the prodigal son a name. I call him Adam, because I think Adam was the first prodigal son. And I believe we can and need to identify with his prodigality. I have also given the "far country" a location. It is east of Eden.

Adam left Eden. He had to, of course. He was driven out. He was driven out by God in one sense and driven out by his choice to sin against God in another sense. So Adam left Eden.

But I don't believe Eden ever left Adam. Everywhere he went there were in his mind comparisons, comparing wherever he was to Eden where once he had lived. Even when he tried every kind of mental discipline he knew to blot out these comparisons, they were there. Everything his senses took in – everything he saw or heard, everything he touched, tasted, or smelled – surely brought comparisons to Eden.

Adam had to forget Eden in order to cope. It was essential that he forget Eden if he was to cope. But if you want my opinion, I don't think Adam ever coped after Eden.

Years ago John Steinbeck wrote a novel entitled, *East of Eden*. It was one of the best-known books written by the famous author. It was made into a movie. I have never read it, and so I have no idea what it was about, but I will tell you what comes to my mind when I hear or see the words, "East of Eden." I am thinking that east of Eden is not Eden, and it doesn't really matter if it is ten thousand miles east or ten feet east. It is still not Eden!

Steinbeck was by no means a religious writer, and he would probably either laugh at you or curse you if you used the word "religious" in his presence. But he must have read the Bible at some time in his life (or maybe it was just luck) because he got the geographical point of reference right when he used the word "east." According to Genesis, when Adam was driven out of Eden, it was to the east, and it was at the eastern gate of Eden where God placed the cherubim and flaming sword to guard the way to the Tree of Life.

What was life like for Adam east of Eden? For one thing, there was the loss of the dignity of work. Work in itself was not a curse or punishment God put upon Adam after Adam was driven from Eden, as some have taught, for God had given Adam a work to do in Eden even before Adam sinned. As a matter of fact, it was the same work whether in Eden or east of Eden: to cultivate the land and to keep it. The difference was that in Eden this work always brought joy and satisfaction. It did not make Adam weary. It gave him no pain, only pleasure. It was as though the land was a toy in the hands of Adam. Something to enjoy. Or, from another perspective, it was a tool or a slave to Adam.

But east of Eden Adam was a slave to the land, and one day the land took Adam. *"Dust you are and to dust you will return"* (Genesis 3:19). The land east of Eden outlived Adam, just as it will outlive you and me.

And before the land took Adam, it spent him. It demanded of him great toil, much sweat of the brow, long hours, and sometimes the pain it gave him was more than he could bear.

There were other characteristics of life east of Eden for Adam and his family. His wife Eve had great pain in giving birth to their children. The children were not born as some curse or punishment to Adam and Eve because of their sin. Just as some err in teaching that work was a punishment, others err in teaching that childbirth was punishment; whereas, the truth is God's command to Adam and Eve to bear children was given before Adam and Eve sinned. It was the pain of childbirth that was punishment. In Eden childbirth would have been painless.

But east of Eden childbirth was painful, and this pain continued after birth. Long after birth. For one of the children of Adam and Eve, Cain, killed his brother Abel. Imagine the pain of that to the parents!

Yet another loss east of Eden was security. East of Eden security became more and more rooted in things: food for today, storing food for tomorrow, shelter, clothes, crude weapons. Things! In Eden security was never in things. It was in the Father God, who met all of Adam's needs. There was in Eden, prior to his sin, never any fear in Adam's heart, for God provided every necessity. The beautiful hymn, "Like a River Glorious," describes what Eden must have been like.

> Like a river glorious is God's perfect peace,
>
> Over all victorious in its bright increase;
>
> Perfect, yet it floweth fuller ev'ry day;
>
> Perfect, yet it groweth deeper all the way.
>
> Hidden in the hollow of his blessed hand,
>
> Never foe can follow, never traitor stand;
>
> Not a surge of worry, not a shade of care,
>
> Not a blast of hurry touch the spirit there.
>
> Stayed upon Jehovah, hearts are fully blest;
>
> Finding, as he promised, perfect peace and rest.

But that was not the security east of Eden. Some have said, including some theologians, that which was lost in Eden because of Adam's sin was

"Innocence." However, what was lost in Eden went far beyond innocence. That which was lost in Eden, Adam and Eve would tell us, was the sound of the footsteps of Someone who once walked in the garden with them and the voice of Someone who once spoke to them in the garden. East of Eden the sound and the voice were no more. You have to call that more than the loss of "innocence."

Satan told Adam and Eve a lie when he told them that if they ate the forbidden fruit, they would become like God. Not only did they not become like God, but they never again became like themselves. So Adam left Eden, but I don't believe Eden ever left Adam.

You and I are modern-day Adams, and we remember Eden, too. We may not be as consciously aware of this remembrance, this longing for Eden, but at our depths we remember Eden, too. As somebody said, "There are only two or three human stories, and they go on repeating themselves just as fiercely as if they had never happened before."

East of Eden work still dominates us. Walter Kerr, the drama critic, said a friend told him he had two fears. One fear was that if he did not slow down, he would have a heart attack. The other was that if he did not hurry up, he would not be able to accomplish enough that was useful before he had his heart attack. I think one naturally laughs when hearing that, but it really is no laughing matter. We are slaves to work!

And for modern-day Eves childbirth is still painful. The nine months of pregnancy have their pain, and the moment of birth is very painful. To give birth mothers either take some sedative at birth to dull the pain, or they spend weeks during their pregnancy going to classes on how to overcome the pain of birth, because childbirth is still painful. In spite of all our modern techniques, inventions, and discoveries, which include putting man on the moon, we still cannot keep the woman from the pain of childbirth!

And the family today still has its problems. In fact, in our nation the family is falling apart. It is being torn asunder. But this is not so surprising, for we live east of Eden.

And east of Eden today, security is still tied to things: life insurance, health insurance, retirement plans, houses, automobiles, guaranteed minimum wage, Social Security, and a thousand other things.

We have so many things in our materialistic age that Adam never had, things that Adam never dreamed would exist, but they have not really brought us joy. And certainly, modern man is more powerful than Adam. In terms of military weapons we have the capacity to blow up the world. Adam didn't even have the capacity to blow up Eden. So modern man is more powerful than Adam, but as Aly Wassil said, "More powerful frustration is the lot of the more powerful."

T. S. Eliot in his verse, *"The Hollow Men,"* described us so well:

We are the hollow men

We are the stuffed men

Leaning together.

Headpiece filled with straw. Alas!

Our dried voices, when

We whisper together

Are quiet and meaningless

As wind in dry grass

Or rats' feet over broken glass

In our dry cellar.

Eliot was right. We are the hollow men. This hollowness caught my eye in a newspaper article that pertained to an interview with a well-known male rock music star on the subject of his steady girl friend. He was asked if he loved her, and he answered, "Yes." He was then asked if he intended to marry her, and the rock star responded by saying he had no intention of marrying her, and he admitted that he had affairs with other women. And then he spoke this sentence which appeared in the newspaper and got my attention: "There are casual relationships which everyone always has, especially in city life." You and I live in that city, and it is a city east of Eden.

In so many ways we really are "the hollow men." Like E. A. Robinson's character, Richard Cory, even the success we seem to enjoy is full of pretense.

…he was rich – yes, richer than a king –

And admirably schooled in every grace:

In fine, we thought that he was everything

To make us wish that we were in his place.

So on we worked, and waited for the light,

And went without meat, and cursed the bread;

And Richard Cory, one calm summer night,

Went home and put a bullet through his head.

We are "the hollow men" who live east of Eden. We miss Eden, too. Don't be afraid to admit that. And don't be ashamed to cry over Eden. It is worth crying over.

Like Adam, we live east of Eden, and like Adam, we still remember Eden. I don't mean we all remember Eden every day, or even every week, or even every year, but we all remember Eden. At the strangest times we remember Eden. Some of these times are when we are so busy with our minds occupied with many things that one would think he would be least likely to remember Eden. But sometimes that is when we most remember Eden. Our busy schedules and crowded calendars cannot keep us from remembering. Some-times we suddenly remember Eden just when we thought we had reached the place where we were so sure Eden was behind us now, something of the past, forgotten forever. Then, suddenly, we remember, like in that song Barbra Streisand sings so well:

Mem'ries light the corners of my mind,

misty watercolor mem'ries of the way we were.[14]

There is absolutely no way that we who live east of Eden can forget Eden. And do you know why? Because the one thing one can never forget is true love. You cannot bury true love deeply enough in your subconscious to forget it.

On God's part, that love is still there. His love has not deserted those of us who live east of Eden. We may be barred from Eden's Tree of Life, but there is an even greater Tree of Life from which we are not barred. The shape of this Tree is the shape of a Cross. That cross even happened east of Eden, which says more about the love of God than all our words. God's only Son died for our sins on that cross. On that cross east of Eden.

Earlier in this message I said that which was lost by man in Eden was far more than "Innocence" and that Adam and Eve would tell you as much. They would say that which was lost in Eden was the sound of Someone who walked in their garden with them and the voice of Someone who once spoke to them in their garden. There came a day, praise God, centuries after Eden when the sound of that Someone walking and the voice of that Someone speaking were heard in another garden. A garden east of Eden. It was in a garden by a tomb. An empty tomb. There in that garden east of Eden a woman named Mary spoke to a stranger she assumed in the pre-dawn to be a gardener, saying to him, *"Sir, if you have carried him away, tell me where you have laid him..."* (John 20:15 RSV).

Then the stranger spoke only one word, her name: *"Mary!"* Life has never been the same since, for since then we have known that the cruelest of men east of Eden in the cruelest of all acts east of Eden could never destroy true love. They crucified it. But it arose and it lives. East of Eden.

The God who would not let ancient Adam (and all of us modern Adams) back into Eden, left Eden himself for us. And those of us who know him through Jesus, our Savior, also know that it is not Eden we long for anyway. It is He!

I have Him. Even east of Eden I have Him!

CHAPTER TWELVE
Pieces
Joel 2:25a KJV

The last chapter of this book is somewhat personal. At some time and in some place in writing about the prodigal son, I realized that I, too, had been a prodigal son.

Maybe that is why I am haunted by the story. No wonder I can't get it out of my mind or out of my heart. This last sermon is about my own prodigality. My fragmented life. The scattered pieces of my heart. It is also about the great grace of the heavenly Father and the power of His grace that found all the scattered pieces of my life and made me whole.

This is my story. Scattered pieces and wholly grace...

A song entitled *"Pieces"* inspired this sermon. I first heard the song many years ago. It moved me very deeply then, and it still does.

Pieces, Pieces, so many pieces to my life.

Scattered all around, and some of them are gone,

and I know that I can't ever

put them back together again.

Pieces, pieces, so many pieces to my life.

A puzzle left unfinished, jumbled and unformed,

who can really ever

fit it all together again?

There are so many pieces to every life. So many pieces. And at times so many pieces seem to be missing. Maybe even most of them.

Life is like a puzzle with a thousand pieces all of which have been tossed up in the wind on a day when the wind is blowing with almost hurricane force so that these pieces scattered in all directions. We don't know where to go to find these pieces. We don't even know where to begin the impossible search. Our lives are so scattered, so fragmented, so broken up in parts. We don't seem to be able to get our lives together.

I think, for example, of my own father now deceased. My dad was an alcoholic, and if there are degrees of alcoholism – and there seem to be – he was one of the most tragic of alcoholics. He was so gifted and so brilliant. Had he stayed away from alcohol, he almost could have owned the town.

I don't doubt that my father loved my mother or that he loved me, but he was never there when a boy needed a dad. Of course, I didn't want him there when he was drunk. I remember so many embarrassing moments because of his drunkenness. Deep scars that took years to heal. But there were other times when he was sober, and I did want him there, but he wasn't there even then because his emotional makeup wouldn't let him. At least, that is what he said. So he didn't show up for my high school, college, and seminary graduations. He missed all the athletic events in which I participated. He skipped my wedding. He was not in the crowd that heard and witnessed my ordination to the ministry. He never heard me preach a single sermon. And I could go on and on…

I loved him and I hated him. I hated him when he stole most of the paper route money I earned one month in order to buy his booze, yet I loved him enough on another occasion to beg Mom not to leave him.

Perhaps the best word to describe what I felt for him is "pity." I pitied him, and I will never forget the most poignant moment of that pity. It happened one morning as I walked out the front door of our home to go to school. There on the front porch I saw Dad. He was just standing there looking out on the field beside the house. He was sober, very sober, yet he looked so forlorn that I said to him, "Dad, what's wrong?" I'll never forget his answer or the look in his eyes as he answered, "I can't get my life together, Sonny. I just can't get it together."

So many pieces to a life. So many scattered pieces. And I don't mean to imply that one has to go through the hell of alcoholism or something similar for his life to be so fragmented that one can't get it together. All of us have a past, part of which we wish we could change. Thomas Jones expressed it with eloquence in a familiar poem.

> Across the fields of yesterday
>
> He sometimes comes to me,
>
> A little lad just back from play—
>
> The lad I used to be.
>
> And yet he smiles so wistfully
>
> Once he has crept within,
>
> I wonder if he hopes to see
>
> The man I might have been?

"The man I might have been." Which one of us does not feel the pathos in that? At times we wonder what we might have been if we had done it differently, made other choices, gone down other roads before the pieces of our lives became so scattered.

We all have a past in which we at some place failed not only ourselves but somebody we loved. Bob Benson tells a story out of his own life, a story which every dad needs to hear. He tells how on the first day of a ten-day vacation he deliberately got up early to go work on the wall down at the lake that was at the foot of his property. He was knee deep in the warm, pleasant water, feeling very content. Patrick, Bob's small son, came down there where his dad was working and asked his dad to teach him how to throw rocks in the water so that they would skip. "In a little while," Bob said to Patrick, "let me get a little more of this wall built."

But after a while Patrick got tired of waiting and started up the hill to the house. Bob figured he would be back quickly, but Patrick didn't come back. Later, when Bob went up for a drink of water, he found Patrick in bed with a high fever which was caused by a very serious illness. Bob, in one of his books, wrote of that incident.

And I can still see him trudging up that hill – a long pull for his short legs but I'm reminded that you never know they're coming back – there aren't any guarantees and the only time you really know you can skip rocks is when you're saying, "in a little while."[15]

So many pieces to a life. So many fragmented pieces. Opportunities gone. Possibilities gone. Chances gone. Choices gone. Love gone. And that is the saddest of all - love gone! That is the hardest piece of life's puzzle to find when it is gone. Mary Webb in a poem described the incredible sorrow of a love that had once come into her life and was gone.

> Why did you come, with your enkindled eyes
>
> And mountain-look, across my lower way,
>
> And take the vague dishonor from my day
>
> By luring me from paltry things, to rise
>
> And stand beside you, waiting wistfully
>
> The looming of a larger destiny?
>
> Why did you with strong fingers fling aside
>
> The gates of possibility, and say
>
> With vital voice the words I dream today?
>
> Before, I was not much unsatisfied:
>
> But since a god has touched me and departed,

I run through every temple broken-hearted.

Love gone! So many pieces. Who could ever find them? Who could even begin to find them?

The pieces of my own life were once so scattered I knew I could not find them. I was equally certain no one else could find them. Yet, the greatest reason I believe in miracles is because someone did find the pieces of my life. Someone found all of them. They were so scattered, so dispersed, so fragmented; yet someone found them. Jesus found them.

I don't know to this day how he found them, because the pieces of my life were so scattered I didn't even think the Son of God could find them. Yet, Jesus found them. I know not how.

But this I do know. He went through hell to find them. For, sometimes, as I pause to see and hear the sights and sounds of life, I see nail prints in hands and a spear wound in a side and a thorn-crowned brow. And now and then, in the midst of night, I hear a terrifying scream: "My God, my God, why have you forsaken me?" Jesus went through hell to find the pieces of my life.

And this I know, too. It was his love for me that led him to search for the pieces of my life. He surely didn't die on the cross in search of the pieces of his life, for his life was never in fragments or pieces. His life is the only perfectly put together life of the ages. So he did not die on the cross to find the pieces of his life. He had them. It was the pieces of my life that were missing. So it could have only been his love that led him to go searching for the pieces of my life. A good and kind Shepherd out in the wilderness looking for the one lost sheep.

And his power that found them had to be a miracle because there was no way the pieces of my life could be found: a frightened little boy of an alcoholic father, a lonely child, a poor teenager, impossible dreams, costly mistakes, failures, sins, illness, crumbling plans, fading hopes, an endless search for love. Those were just some of the scattered pieces of my life. They just could not be found. Yet Jesus found them. All of them!

You may not know how much this means to me unless you, too, have lost the pieces of your life. I think sometimes we forget that Jesus didn't just come to save us for the future of heaven. He also came to make us whole today. You may need his wholeness today as much as you need his heaven tomorrow. Because there are so many missing pieces in your life.

This chapter has a biblical text at its beginning. It is part of a verse found in the prophet Joel in which God speaks. I am aware of the fact that thus far in the sermon I have not addressed this text. You might think it is a questionable text anyway. In the text God says, *"I will restore to you the years that the locust hath eaten."* The context refers to the destruction of the crops of Hebrew people by locusts, which might not seem like the greatest need or problem in our world today. After all, there are bigger problems: cancer, divorce, depression, death, loneliness, AIDS.

Big problems. Great needs.

But read the verse in Joel again and take out the word "locust," and in its place put in the word that most relates to your own most desperate need. *"I will restore to you the years that the _____ hath eaten."* Who but God can give back the years?

Some time ago, I heard a true story about a young divorced woman who went one afternoon to visit her father in his home nearby. It was a moment when she was feeling very low and discouraged. Her main reason for going to her father's home that day was the hope that he might have an encouraging word to lift her spirit. Her dad, however, who was normally very attentive to her words and feelings, was preoccupied with something else, so she did not get the sympathetic ear she desired.

In anger and disgust she said, "I tell you, you could take all the happiness in this world and cram it into twenty minutes!" To this her father replied, "It would be a beautiful twenty minutes."

That is profoundly true. In spite of the many sorrows and great hurts in life, if you could take all the happiness in this world – the best of all the happy moments of any one of us – and cram it into twenty minutes, it would be a beautiful twenty minutes.

The God revealed in Jesus intends to give us more than twenty minutes out of the best years of our lives. He has promised us the gift of eternity. One day in a land called heaven, when at last we see God with our own eyes, perhaps the greatest surprise will be that in that moment He will give us all the pieces of our lives.

Who but God can give back the years? Somewhere between Calvary and the empty tomb Jesus found all the pieces of our lives. If you will let him, he will make you whole. I know because he has made me whole. Whoever could believe that a Carpenter would find all the pieces of my life?

NOTES

1   **James W. Moore,** *You Can Get Bitter or Better!*
    (Nashville: Abingdon Press, 1989), pp. 70-71.

2   **H. Stephen Shoemaker,** *God Stories*
    (Valley Forge, PA: Judson Press, 1998), p.250.

3   **This story about Sybil Canon is told by J. Ellsworth Kalas,**
    Parables from the Back Side (Nashville: Abingdon Press, 1992), p.83.

4   **C. S. Lewis,** *Mere Christianity*
    (New York: The MacMillan Company, 1958), p.39.

5   **This story about two brothers is told by Brennan Manning,**
    Lion and Lamb **(Old Tappan, NJ: Fleming H. Revell Company,
    1986), pp.135-136**

6   **Henri J. M. Nouwen,** *The Return of the Prodigal Son*
    (New York: Doubleday, 1992), p.32.

7   *The Washington Post,* **June 18, 1994.**

8   **Sam Keen,** *The Passionate Life*
    (San Francisco: Harper Collins Publishers, 1983), p.191.

9   **This story by O. Henry is cited in John Bishop,** *A Word in Season*
    (Nashville: Abingdon, 1979), pp.34-35.

10 **Cited in Charles R. Swindoll,** *Come Before Winter*
    (Portland, Oregon: Multnomah Press, 1985), pp.36-37.

11 **Frederick Buechner,** *The Final Beast*
    (San Francisco: Harper & Row, Publishers, 1965), p.115.

12 **George Byron, cited in George A. Buttrick,** *The Parables of Jesus*
    (Grand Rapids, Michigan: Baker Book House, 1973), p.255.

13 **Alan Paton,** *Cry, the Beloved Country*
    (New York: Charles Scribner's Sons, 1948), pp. 124-125.

14 **Lines from "The Way We Were." Words by Alan Bergman;
    Music by Marvin Hamlisch. Copyright 1973.**

15 **Bob Benson,** *Come Share The Being*
    (Nashville: Impact Books, 1974), p.99

ABOUT THE AUTHOR

Lewis N. McDonald is a retired pastor with pastorates in Texas and Maryland. He lives with his wife Patsy in Chestertown, Maryland.

McDonald served as pastor of South Avenue Baptist Church, Pasadena, Texas, from 1965-1971, Oak Grove Baptist Church, Bel Air, Maryland, as minister of preaching from 1971-1989 and as pastor of Memorial United Methodist Church, Poolesville, Maryland, from 1991-2002.

He has been listed in Who's Who in America, Personalities of America, International Platform Association, International Men of Achievement and Notable Americans.

McDonald is a recipient of "Key of the City" of Pasadena, Texas, for pastoring in Pasadena from 1965-1971.

He has served as a trustee of Southwestern Baptist Theological Seminary (1979-1989), president of the Baptist Convention of Maryland/Delaware (1980-1982), and represented Protestants in America at the celebration of 350 years of Catholicism in America (1982).

CPSIA information can be obtained at www.ICGtesting.com
Printed in the USA
239448LV00001B/146/P